بسم الله الرحمن الرحيم

PRAYERS UPON THE BELOVED

SUPPLICATIONS BY ALLAH'S MOST BEAUTIFUL NAMES FOR THE ONE WHO HAD THE MOST BEAUTIFUL TRAITS

والله

يعطي إنما أنا

قاسم

الحديث

Prayers upon the Beloved

SUPPLICATIONS BY ALLAH'S MOST BEAUTIFUL NAMES
FOR THE ONE WHO HAD THE MOST BEAUTIFUL TRAITS

Author
ḤABĪB ʿUMAR B. ḤAFĪẒ

Translation & Notes
ABDULLAH SALIH

Title:
PRAYERS ON THE BELOVED:
SUPPLICATIONS BY ALLAH'S MOST BEAUTIFUL NAMES
FOR THE ONE WHO HAD THE MOST BEAUTIFUL TRAITS

ISBN:
978-1-952306-04-4 (paperback)
978-1-952306-12-9 (hardback)

FIRST EDITION | NOVEMBER 2020

Author:
ḤABĪB ʿUMAR BIN ḤAFĪẒ

Translator:
ABDULLAH SALIH

Typeset:
IMRAN RAHIM

Imam Ghazali
INSTITUTE

Contents

Foreword
I

Translator's Introduction
III

The Author
V

Prayers Upon the Beloved
1

APPENDIX 1:
Insights into Sending Prayers Upon the Prophet ﷺ
85

APPENDIX 2:
Being with Allah ﷻ and His Messenger ﷺ
89

Foreword

In the name of Allah, the Most Compassionate, the Most Merciful

SENDING PRAYERS UPON OUR MASTER, Muhammad ﷺ is one of the greatest means of drawing close to Allah Most High. Many independent works have delineated its virtues and benefits. In Ahmad Farid al-Mazidi's foreword to Shaykh Muhy al-Din ibn Arabi's *Kashf al-asrar li salah sayyid al-abrar*, he listed nearly two hundred such works. One of the early works in this regard is *Fadl al-salah ala al-nabi* (The virtue of sending prayers upon the Prophet) by Al-Hafiẓ Isma'il bin Ishaq. More well-known compilations include *Al-Qawl al-badi fi al-salah ala al-Ḥabīb al-shafi* by Imam al-Sakhawi and *Al-Durr al-mandud fi al-salah ala sahib al-maqam al-mahmud* by Ibn Hajar al-Haytami. These virtues and benefits include:

1. removing worry and anxiety;
2. erasing sins;
3. being showered in Allah's Mercy;
4. being favoured with proximity to the Prophet on the Day of Judgment;
5. establishing one's feet on the bridge leading over hellfire;
6. being honoured with the company of Allah's Beloved in Paradise.

One of the innovations of our time is the creation of a dichotomy between Allah ﷻ and His Messenger ﷺ. Imbued with an ideology foreign to the way of Ahl al-Sunnah, the proponents of this innovation have impressed upon people that the Prophet ﷺ should not be praised too often, or too much, and that the remembrance of him should not be equated with the remembrance of Allah ﷻ. When I was in a taxi once, the driver said, "I find so much enjoyment in sending prayers upon the Prophet, but I was told I should actually be spending more time engaging in the remembrance of Allah ﷻ. Am I sinful by spending more time sending prayers upon Allah's Prophet?" I replied to him saying, "Not at all. The Prophet ﷺ is not to be placed alongside Allah, such that you either remember him or you remember Allah ﷻ. He ﷺ falls under Allah and therefore whenever one remembers him, one remembers Allah ﷻ. In fact, one cannot send prayers upon the Prophet without calling out, remembering and mentioning one of the Names of Allah Most High.

This compilation by our teacher and spiritual guide, sayyidi al-Ḥabīb Umar bin Hafīẓ, is unique in that each form of prayer highlights the connection between the Messenger ﷺ and the Names and Qualities of Allah ﷻ. In addition, each form includes a unique supplication for the one reciting it. The reciter of these prayers thus finds himself engaging in the remembrance of Allah ﷻ by calling Him through His Most Sublime Names, and asking Him to send prayers and increase the honour and rank of the Messenger ﷺ. By doing this, he obtains the virtues and reward of sending prayers upon the Prophet, and also supplicates to Allah ﷻ, asking Him such amazing things that we are generally unable to think of when asking of Him.

One should note that while these forms may not have been transmitted directly from the Messenger ﷺ, they have been compiled by one of his true and complete descendants. Saints are usually inspired by Allah ﷻ when formulating such prayers, and we believe that this compilation is the fruit of such inspiration.

May Allah ﷻ bless and reward our brother, Abdullah Salih, for his effort in rendering this invaluable compilation into English. May He accept the intentions of the publisher and cause this work to benefit the ummah and encourage them to grow in love for Allah's final Messenger ﷺ. May we all come to follow the Muhammadan way closely. *Amin.*

[SHAYKH] ABDURRAGMAAN KHAN
22 RAMADAN 1441 | 16 MAY 2020

Translator's Introduction

All praise is due to Allah ﷻ, the First, Who is without a beginning and the Last, Who is without an end. Prayers and Peace be upon the Prophet Muhammad ﷺ, the first Prophet on the Day of Judgment to offer intercession despite being the last Prophet sent, and upon his pure family, his blessed companions, and all who follow their way upon the path of righteousness, until the day when intercession will begin with none other than the Prophet Muhammad ﷺ.

By way of introduction, to that which does not require an introduction, we mention a beautiful Hadith, which begins with a question, continues with a resolution, and concludes with Prophetic glad tidings for the questioner specifically, and in general, for all those who send abundant prayers upon the Prophet Muhammad ﷺ.

A companion by the name of Ubayy bin Ka'b, may Allah be well pleased with him, said to the Prophet Muhammad ﷺ: "O Messenger of Allah, I desire to send abundant prayers upon you, so how much [of my time] should I apportion for you?" The Prophet ﷺ responded: "Whatever you desire." The companion suggested: "A fourth? [of my time]" The Prophet ﷺ responded: "Whatever you desire, but if you increase, then it is better for you." The companion further suggested: "Half? [of my time]" The Prophet ﷺ responded: "Whatever you desire, but if you increase, then it is better for you." The companion further suggested: "Two thirds? [of my time]" The Prophet ﷺ responded: "Whatever you desire, but if you increase, then it is better for you." The companion resolutely suggested: "I shall use all of my time." The Prophet ﷺ responded with glad tidings and said: "[If this is the case] Then all your concerns will be resolved, and all your sins will be forgiven." May Allah ﷻ allow us all to be among those who send abundant prayers upon the Prophet Muhammad ﷺ.

This Hadith, together with many others, enlightens us about the virtuous act of sending prayers upon the Prophet Muhammad ﷺ. One is not required to be in a state of ritual purity in order to send prayers upon the Prophet ﷺ, though if you are in a state of ritual purity, then the better it is for you. One is not required to have a certain level of knowledge about the Prophet Muhammad ﷺ in order to send prayers upon him ﷺ, though the more you know about the one upon whom you are sending prayers, then the better it is for you. The act of sending prayers upon him ﷺ is not restricted to a particular time, though if you send prayers upon him ﷺ at a time when you are focused and undistracted, then the better it is for you. The act of sending prayers upon him ﷺ is not restricted to a particular quantity, though if you send prayers upon him ﷺ in abundance, then the better it is for you. May Allah ﷻ allow us all, within our lives, homes, and daily affairs, to be of those who bring to life and implement this virtuous act of sending abundant prayers upon the Prophet Muhammad ﷺ.

Let us regularly ask ourselves where we stand in relation to the Prophetic glad tidings of the aforementioned Hadith, and what our portion thereof is? During our year, that consists of 12 months, how many months therein have we dedicated and committed towards performing this virtuous act of sending prayers upon the Prophet Muhammad ﷺ? During our months, weeks, days, hours, minutes and seconds, how much time have we set aside and allocated towards this virtuous act of sending prayers upon the Prophet Muhammad ﷺ? The answers to such questions are a direct indication of one's level of connection, in this life, and most importantly in the Hereafter, to the Prophet Muhammad ﷺ.

In conclusion, what follows is a booklet which despite being small in size, is indeed great in virtue. We ask Allah ﷻ to generously accept all those who read it, and ask Him to make it a means by which we attain success on the day when intercession will begin with none other than the Prophet Muhammad ﷺ.

The Author

HABĪB ʿUMAR B. HAFĪẒ

HIS LINEAGE

Ḥabīb ʿUmar was born in Tarim, in Yemen's Hadramawt Valley. He is a direct descendant of the Messenger of Allah ﷺ through Imam al-Husayn. His father and his father's father and all his forefathers were scholars and knowers of Allah. Among his blessed forefathers are Imam ʿAli Zayn al-ʿAbidin as well as the first of the Prophetic Household to settle in Hadramawt, Imam Ahmad bin ʿIsa al-Muhajir and his noble descendants, al-Faqih al-Muqaddam Muhammad bin ʿAli, Shaykh ʿAbd al-Rahman al-Saqqaf and Shaykh Abu Bakr bin Salim. His full lineage is as follows:

He is al-Ḥabīb al-ʿAllamah ʿUmar bin Muhammad bin Salim bin Hafīẓ bin ʿAbdullah bin Abu Bakr bin ʿAydarus bin ʿUmar bin ʿAydarus bin ʿUmar bin Abu Bakr bin ʿAydarus bin al-Husayn bin al-Shaykh al-Fakhr Abu Bakr bin Salim bin ʿAbdullah bin ʿAbd al-Rahman bin ʿAbdullah bin Shaykh ʿAbd al-Rahman al-Saqqaf bin Shaykh Muḥammad Mawla al-Dawilah, bin ʿAli Mawla al-Darak, bin ʿAlawi al-Ghayur, bin al-Faqih al-Muqaddam Muhammad, bin ʿAli, bin Muhammad Sahib Mirbat, bin ʿAli Khaliʿ Qasam, bin ʿAlawi, bin Muhammad Sahib al-Sawmaʿah, bin ʿAlawi, bin ʿUbaydullah, bin al-Imam al-Muhajir il-Allah Ahmad, bin ʿIsa, bin Muhammad al-Naqib, bin ʿAli al-ʿUraydi, bin Jaʿfar al-Sadiq, bin Muhammad al-Baqir, bin ʿAli Zayn al-ʿAbidin, bin Husayn al-Sibt, bin ʿAli bin Abi Talib and Fatimah al-Zahra', the daughter of our Master Muhammad, the Seal of the Prophets ﷺ.

HIS STUDY OF THE ISLAMIC SCIENCES

At an early age, Ḥabīb ʿUmar memorized the Qur'an and began studying the Islamic sciences under his father and many of the great scholars of Tarim of the time. Among them were Ḥabīb Muhammad bin ʿAlawi bin Shihab, Ḥabīb Ahmad bin ʿAli Ibn Shaykh Abu Bakr,

Ḥabīb ʿAbdullah bin Shaykh al-ʿAydarus, Ḥabīb ʿAbdullah bin Hasan Balfaqih, Ḥabīb ʿUmar bin ʿAlawi al-Kaf, Ḥabīb Ahmad bin Hasan al-Haddad, Ḥabīb Hasan bin ʿAbdullah al-Shatiri and his brother, Ḥabīb Salim, the Mufti, Shaykh Fadl bin ʿAbd al-Rahman Ba Fadl, and Shaykh Tawfiq Aman. He also studied under his older brother, Ḥabīb ʿAli al-Mashhur, who was the Mufti of Tarim.

HIS MIGRATION TO AL-BAYDA'

In 1387 (1967), a socialist government came to power in South Yemen which attempted to eradicate Islam from society. Scholars were persecuted and religious institutions were forcibly closed. In spite of this, Ḥabīb ʿUmar's father, Ḥabīb Muhammad, fearlessly continued calling people to Allah. He was required to register with the security forces on a regular basis so that they could check on his whereabouts. Thus, on Friday morning on 29th Dhu'l-Hijjah 1392 (1973) he left Ḥabīb ʿUmar, then only nine years of age, in the mosque before the Friday prayer and went to register. He was never seen again. Ḥabīb ʿUmar remained in Tarim under the care of his blessed mother, Hababah Zahra bint Hafīẓ al-Haddar and his older brother, Ḥabīb ʿAli al-Mashhur. The situation in Hadramawt became increasingly difficult and thus in Safar 1402 (1981), Ḥabīb ʿUmar migrated to the city of al-Bayda' in North Yemen, safe from the socialist regime in South Yemen.

He resided in the Ribat of al-Bayda' and studied at the hands of the founder of the Ribat, the great Imam, Ḥabīb Muhammad bin ʿAbdullah al-Haddar, as well as Ḥabīb Zayn bin Ibrahim bin Sumayt, the Ribat's main teacher. Ḥabīb Muhammad held him in high regard and could see the future that was awaiting him. He duly married his daughter to him. Ḥabīb ʿUmar inherited his father's passion for teaching people and calling them to Allah ﷻ, and he had begun this noble work at the age of fifteen, but it was in al-Bayda that he had the opportunity to work freely. He had a great impact on the youth of the city and was a means for many of them to become students in the Ribat and then scholars and callers to Allah ﷻ. He established a number of weekly lessons and gatherings of knowledge. He would often travel in order to call to Allah ﷻ in the area around of al-Bayda', just as he would travel further afield to al-Hudaydah and Taʿizz. He used to frequently visit Taʿizz in order to take knowledge from the great scholar, Ḥabīb Ibrahim bin ʿAqil bin Yahya.

HIS REPEATED VISITS TO THE HIJAZ

During his time in al-Bayda', Ḥabīb ᶜUmar made frequent visits to the Hijaz. There he learnt from the great Imams of the time: Ḥabīb ᶜAbd al-Qadir al-Saqqaf, Ḥabīb Ahmad Mashhur al-Haddad, and Ḥabīb ᶜAbu Bakr al-Attas al-Habashi. He took license to narrate from the chains of transmission in Hadith and in other sciences from Shaykh Muhammad Yasin al-Faddani and the Hadith scholar of the Two Sanctuaries, Sayyid Muhammad bin ᶜAlawi al-Maliki, as well as other scholars.

HIS MOVE TO OMAN AND AL-SHIHR

After the fall of the socialist regime in 1410 (1990) and the unification of North and South Yemen, Ḥabīb ᶜUmar returned to Hadramawt. He visited Tarim, and then settled with some of his students in city of Salalah in the Sultanate of Oman. For a year and a half he called people to Allah in the region and then in 1413 (1992) he moved to the city of al-Shihr, which lies on the Indian Ocean in the province of Hadramawt. The Ribat of al-Mustafa had recently been reopened after closure during the days of the socialist regime. Ḥabīb ᶜUmar began teaching in the Ribat and reviving its traditions. Many students from different regions of Yemen and parts of South-East Asia came to seek knowledge from him.

HIS RETURN TO TARIM

Ḥabīb ᶜUmar then returned to his home city and immediately began to breathe new life into the religious life of the region. His tireless work led to the establishment of Dar al-Mustafa in 1414 (1994). Dar al-Mustafa is a centre for traditional Islamic learning based upon three foundations: the first is *ᶜilm* (knowledge), learning the sciences of the Sacred Law from those who are qualified to impart them through connected chains of transmission; the second is *tazkiyah,* purifying the soul and refining one's character and the third is *daᶜwah,* calling to Allah and conveying beneficial knowledge. Dar al-Mustafa began in Ḥabīb ᶜUmar's house next to the Mawla ᶜAidid mosque and a batch of students from South East Asia came to study with him, as well as students from Tarim and other parts of Yemen. As the number of students increased, the need for a purpose-built building became clear. Land was duly purchased and building started. Dar al-Mustafa was officially opened in 1417 (1997). Ḥabīb ᶜUmar honored his father's sacrifice by making the opening date 29th Dhu'l-Hijjah, the day on which Ḥabīb Muhammad was abducted. Although Dar al-Mustafa was established recently, it is intimately connected to the illustrious legacy of the scholarly tradition of Hadramawt, which stretches back more than a thousand years. In this we witness the renewal of the religion (*tajdid*) that is taking place at the hands of Ḥabīb ʿUmar.

Dar al-Zahra' was opened in 1422 (2001) to provide learning opportunities for women as well. A number of branches of Dar al-Mustafa have since been opened in Hadramawt and South East Asia. A branch has been opened in the Yemeni capital, Sanʿa', and older ribats have also been revived, such as the ribats of al-Shihr, Mukalla' and ʿAynat. Dar al-Mustafa and its branches continue to grow and receive students from all corners of the earth.

HIS TRAVELS

Ḥabīb ʿUmar constantly travels to convey the Prophetic message and to call people to Allah. He delivers regular lectures and *khutbahs* within Hadramawt and often makes trips abroad. His travels have taken him to almost all the Arab states, East and South Africa, South East Asia and Australia, the Indian Subcontinent, Western Europe and Scandinavia and North America. He has connected to the chains of transmission of the scholars of these regions and has also participated in many Islamic conferences.

HIS WRITINGS AND PUBLICATIONS

Although Ḥabīb ʿUmar is best known for his speeches and lessons, he has authored several works. Among them are *al-Dhakirah al-Musharrafah,* which contains personally obligatory knowledge for every Muslim, and three short hadith compilations, *Mukhtar al-Hadith*, *Nur al-Iman* and *Qutuf al-Falihin*. His *Qabas al-Nur al-Mubin* is a summarised version of the third quarter of Imam al-Ghazali's *Ihya' ʿUlum al-Din* and is an expression of his concern for curing the ailments of the heart. It also reflects the love and respect that the Ba ʿAlawi scholars have traditionally had for *Ihya' ʿUlum al-Din.* A selection of Ḥabīb ʿUmar's speeches and wisdoms have been collected in *Tawjihat al-Tullab* and *Tawjih al-Nabih,* and some of his *khutbahs* have been collected in *Fayd al-Imdad. Khulasat al-Madad al-Nabawi* is Ḥabīb ʿUmar's compilation of *adhkar* for the seeker to recite on a daily basis. It contains Prophetic invocations and the litanies of many of the great Imams. His mawlid compositions, *al-Diya' al-Lami'* and *al-Sharab al-Tahur* are recited in gatherings throughout the world, as are his poems.

والله يعطي

إنما أنا قاسم

الحديث

Prayers upon the Beloved

SUPPLICATIONS BY ALLAH'S MOST BEAUTIFUL NAMES
FOR THE ONE WHO HAD THE MOST BEAUTIFUL TRAITS

Author
ḤABĪB ʿUMAR B. ḤAFĪẒ

Translation & Notes
ABDULLAH SALIH

أعوذ بالله من الشيطان الرجيم

I seek refuge with Allah from the accursed Satan

بسم الله الرحمن الرحيم

In the Name of Allah,
the Most Compassionate, the Most Merciful

إن الله وملائكته يصلون على النبي
يا أيها الذين آمنوا صلوا عليه وسلموا تسليما

Verily, Allah and His Angels send prayers upon the Prophet;
O you who believe, send prayers and peace upon him

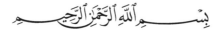

ٱللّٰهُمَّ يَا ٱللّٰهُ يَا رَحْمَٰنُ يَا رَحِيمُ صَلِّ عَلَىٰ عَبْدِكَ
وَحَبِيبِكَ سَيِّدِنَا مُحَمَّدٍ ٱلنَّبِيِّ ٱلرَّحِيمِ وَعَلَىٰ آلِهِ
وَصَحْبِهِ وَسَلِّمْ تَسْلِيمًا وَارْحَمْنِي بِهِ رَحْمَةً وَاسِعَةً

Allāhumma yā Allāh yā Raḥmān yā Raḥīm ṣalli ʿalā ʿabdika wa ḥabībika sayyidinā Muḥammad al-nabiyy al-rahīm wa ʿalā ālihi wa ṣaḥbihi wa sallim taslīman war-ḥamnī bihi raḥmatan wāsiʿah

O Allah, O Most Compassionate, O Most Merciful, send prayers and abundant Peace upon Your slave and beloved, our master, Muhammad, the merciful Prophet and upon his family and companions, and through him, have abundant mercy upon me

NUMBER TWO

اَللّٰهُمَّ يَا اَللّٰهُ يَا قُدُّوسُ صَلِّ عَلَىٰ عَبْدِكَ وَحَبِيبِكَ
سَيِّدِنَا مُحَمَّدٍ ٱلنَّبِيِّ ٱلْمُقَدَّسِ وَعَلَىٰ آلِهِ وَصَحْبِهِ وَسَلِّمْ
تَسْلِيمًا وَقَدِّسْنِي بِهِ تَقْدِيسًا

Allāhumma yā Allāh yā Quddūs ṣalli ʿalā ʿabdika wa ḥabībika sayyidinā Muḥammad al-nabiyy al-muqaddas wa ʿalā ālihi wa ṣaḥbihi wa sallim taslīman wa qaddisnī bihi taqdīsā

O Allah, O Most Pure, send prayers and abundant Peace upon Your slave and beloved, our master, Muhammad, the purified Prophet, and upon his family and companions, and through him, purify me completely

اَللّٰهُمَّ يَا اَللّٰهُ يَا سَلَامُ صَلِّ عَلَىٰ عَبْدِكَ وَحَبِيبِكَ
سَيِّدِنَا مُحَمَّدٍ اَلنَّبِيِّ اَلسَّلَامِ وَعَلَىٰ آلِهِ وَصَحْبِهِ وَسَلِّمْ
تَسْلِيمًا وَسَلِّمْنِي بِهِ وَلَقِّنِي بِهِ تَحِيَّةً وَسَلَامًا

Allāhumma yā Allāh yā Salām ṣalli ʿalā ʿabdika wa ḥabībika sayyidinā Muḥammad al-nabiyy al-salām wa ʿalā ālihi wa ṣaḥbihi wa sallim taslīman wa sallimnī bihi wa laqqinī bihi taḥiyyatan wa salāmā

O Allah, O Giver of peace, send prayers and abundant Peace upon Your slave and beloved, our master, Muhammad, the Prophet of peace, and upon his family and companions, and through him, grant me peace, protect me and receive me with greetings and peace

NUMBER FOUR

ٱللَّٰهُمَّ يَا ٱللهُ يَا مُؤْمِنُ صَلِّ عَلَىٰ عَبْدِكَ وَحَبِيبِكَ
سَيِّدِنَا مُحَمَّدٍ ٱلنَّبِيِّ ٱلْمُؤْمِنِ وَعَلَىٰ آلِهِ وَصَحْبِهِ وَسَلِّمْ
تَسْلِيمًا وَزِدْنِي بِهِ فِي كُلِّ نَفَسٍ إِيمَانًا

Allāhumma yā Allāh yā Mu'min ṣalli 'alā 'abdika wa ḥabībika sayyidinā Muḥammad al-nabiyy al-mu'min wa 'alā ālihi wa ṣaḥbihi wa sallim taslīman wa zidnī bihi fī kulli nafasin īmānā

O Allah, O Giver of faith, send prayers and abundant Peace upon Your slave and beloved, our master, Muhammad, the faithful Prophet, and upon his family and companions, and through him, increase me in faith with every breath that I take

ٱللَّهُمَّ يَا ٱللَّهُ يَا عَزِيزُ صَلِّ عَلَىٰ عَبْدِكَ وَحَبِيبِكَ
سَيِّدِنَا مُحَمَّدٍ ٱلنَّبِيِّ ٱلْعَزِيزِ وَعَلَىٰ آلِهِ وَصَحْبِهِ وَسَلِّمْ
تَسْلِيمًا وَأَعِزْنِي بِهِ وَاجْعَلْ لِي بِطَاعَتِكَ وَقُرْبِكَ عِزًّا

Allāhumma yā Allāh yā ʿAzīz ṣalli ʿalā ʿabdika wa ḥabībika sayyidinā Muḥammad al-nabiyyi al-ʿazīz wa ʿalā ālihi wa ṣaḥbihi wa sallim taslīman wa aʿiznī bihī wajʿal lī biṭāʿatika wa qurbika ʿizzā

O Allah, O Powerful One, send prayers and abundant Peace upon Your slave and beloved, our master, Muhammad, the powerful Prophet, and upon his family and companions, and through him, grant me power, and make me, through Your obedience and proximity, powerful

ٱللَّهُمَّ يَا ٱللهُ يَا مُتَكَبِّرُ صَلِّ عَلَىٰ عَبْدِكَ وَحَبِيبِكَ
سَيِّدِنَا مُحَمَّدٍ ٱلنَّبِيِّ أَعْظَمِ ٱلْخَلْقِ تَوَاضُعًا لَكَ وَعَلَىٰ
آلِهِ وَصَحْبِهِ وَسَلِّمْ تَسْلِيمًا وَنَقِّنِي بِهِ عَنْ شَوَائِبِ
ٱلْكِبْرِ وَارْزُقْنِي تَوَاضُعًا عَظِيمًا

Allāhumma yā Allāh yā Mutakabbir ṣalli ʿalā ʿabdika wa ḥabībika sayyidinā Muḥammad al-nabiyy aʿẓam il-khalq tawāḍuʿan laka wa ʿalā ālihi wa ṣaḥbihi wa sallim taslīman wa naqqinī bihi ʿan shawāʾib il-kibr war-zuqnī tawāḍuʿan ʿaẓīmā

O Allah, O Supreme One, send prayers and abundant Peace upon Your slave and beloved, our master, Muhammad, the most humble of creation in Your presence, and upon his family and companions, and cleanse me, through him, from the stains of arrogance, and endow me with great humility

ٱللّٰهُمَّ يَا ٱللّٰهُ يَا خَالِقُ صَلِّ عَلَىٰ عَبْدِكَ وَحَبِيبِكَ
سَيِّدِنَا مُحَمَّدٍ ٱلنَّبِيِّ أَكْرَمِ خَلْقِكَ وَأَسْعَدِ مَخْلُوقَاتِكَ
وَعَلَىٰ آلِهِ وَصَحْبِهِ وَسَلِّمْ تَسْلِيمًا وَحَسِّنْ بِهِ خَلْقِي
وَخُلُقِي فَضْلًا وَإِحْسَانًا

Allāhumma yā Allāh yā Khāliq ṣalli ʿalā ʿabdika wa ḥabībika sayyidinā Muhammadin al-nabiyy akrami khalqika wa mahklūqātika wa ʿalā ālihi wa ṣaḥbihi wa sallim taslīman wa ḥassin bihi khalqī wa khuluqī faḍlan wa iḥsānā

O Allah, O Creator, send prayers and abundant Peace upon Your slave and beloved, our master, Muhammad, the Prophet who is the most honorable and successful of Your creation, and upon his family and companions, and beautify, through him, my appearance and character with favor and beneficence

NUMBER EIGHT

ٱللّٰهُمَّ يَا ٱللّٰهُ يَا بَارِئُ صَلِّ عَلَىٰ عَبْدِكَ وَحَبِيبِكَ
سَيِّدِنَا مُحَمَّدٍ ٱلنَّبِيِّ أَكْرَمِ مَنْ بَرَأْتَ وَعَلَىٰ آلِهِ
وَصَحْبِهِ وَسَلِّمْ تَسْلِيمًا وَأَثْبِتْنِي عِنْدَكَ فِي خَيْرِ
ٱلْبَرِيَّةِ فَضْلًا وَإِحْسَانًا

Allāhumma yā Allāh yā Bāri' ṣalli 'alā 'abdika wa ḥabībika sayyidinā Muḥammad al-nabiyy akrami man bara'ta wa 'alā ālihi wa ṣaḥbihi wa sallim taslīman wa athbitnī 'indaka fī khayr il-bariyyah faḍlan wa iḥsānā

O Allah, O Originator, send prayers and abundant Peace upon Your slave and beloved, our master, Muhammad, the Prophet who is the most honorable of whom You created, and upon his family and companions, and establish me, through him, in Your presence, with the best of Your creation with favor and beneficence

ٱللَّهُمَّ يَا ٱللَّهُ يَا مُصَوِّرُ صَلِّ عَلَىٰ عَبْدِكَ وَحَبِيبِكَ
سَيِّدِنَا مُحَمَّدٍ ٱلنَّبِيِّ أَجْمَلِ وَأَكْمَلِ مَنْ صَوَّرْتَ وَعَلَىٰ
آلِهِ وَصَحْبِهِ وَسَلِّمْ تَسْلِيمًا وَاجْعَلْنِي بِهِ أَلْقَاكَ عَلَىٰ أَجْمَلِ
صُورَةٍ يَلْقَاكَ بِهَا ٱلْمُقَرَّبُونَ إِلَيْكَ جُودًا وَامْتِنَانًا

Allāhumma yā Allāh yā Muṣawwir ṣalli ʿalā ʿabdika wa ḥabībika sayyidinā Muḥammad al-nabiyy ajmali wa akmali man ṣawwarta wa ʿalā ālihi wa ṣaḥbihi wa sallim taslīman wajʿalnī bihi alqāka ʿalā ajmali ṣūratin yalqāka bihā al-muqarrabūna ilayka jūdan wamtinānā

O Allah, O Fashioner, send prayers and abundant Peace upon Your slave and beloved, our master, Muhammad, the Prophet who is the most beautiful and complete of whom You fashioned, and make me, through him, to meet You in the most beautiful of forms in which You are met by those who are close to You, with generosity and kindness

ٱللّٰهُمَّ يَا ٱللّٰهُ يَا غَفَّارُ صَلِّ عَلَىٰ عَبْدِكَ وَحَبِيبِكَ
سَيِّدِنَا مُحَمَّدٍ ٱلنَّبِيِّ مِفْتَاحِ بَابِ مَغْفِرَتِكَ وَعَلَىٰ آلِهِ
وَصَحْبِهِ وَسَلِّمْ تَسْلِيمًا وَاغْفِرْلِي بِهِ مَا تَقَدَّمَ مِنْ ذَنْبِي
وَمَا تَأَخَّرَ غُفْرَانًا

Allāhumma yā Allāh yā Ghaffār ṣalli ʿalā ʿabdika wa ḥabībika sayyidinā Muḥammad al-nabiyy miftāhi bābi maghfiratika wa ʿalā ālihi wa ṣaḥbihi wa sallim taslīman waghfirlī bihi mā taqaddama min dhanbi wa mā ta'akhkhara ghufrānā

O Allah, O Forgiving One, send prayers and abundant Peace upon Your slave and beloved, our master, Muhammad, the Prophet who is the key to the door of Your forgiveness, and upon his family and companions, and through him, forgive my past and future sins completely

ٱللّٰهُمَّ يَا ٱللّٰهُ يَا وَهَّابُ صَلِّ عَلَىٰ عَبْدِكَ وَحَبِيبِكَ
سَيِّدِنَا مُحَمَّدٍ ٱلنَّبِيِّ مِفْتَاحِ بَابِ ٱلْمَوَاهِبِ وَعَلَىٰ آلِهِ
وَصَحْبِهِ وَسَلِّمْ تَسْلِيمًا وَهَبْ لِي بِهِ مِنْ مَوَاهِبِكَ مَا
أَنْتَ أَهْلُهُ فَضْلًا وَإِحْسَانًا

Allāhumma yā Allāh yā Wahhāb ṣalli ʿalā ʿabdika wa ḥabībika sayyidinā Muḥammad al-nabiyy miftāhi bābi il-mawāhib wa ʿalā ālihi wa ṣaḥbihi wa sallim taslīman wa hab lī bihi min mawāhibika mā anta ahluhu faḍlan wa iḥsānā

O Allah, O Giver, send prayers and abundant Peace upon Your slave and beloved, our master, Muhammad, the Prophet who is the key to the door of Your gifts, and upon his family and companions, and through him, gift me from Your gifts, with the grace and generosity of which only You are capable of doing

ٱللَّٰهُمَّ يَا ٱللَّٰهُ يَا رَزَّاقُ صَلِّ عَلَىٰ عَبْدِكَ وَحَبِيبِكَ سَيِّدِنَا
مُحَمَّدٍ ٱلنَّبِيِّ وَاسِطَةِ ٱلْأَرْزَاقِ وَعَلَىٰ آلِهِ وَصَحْبِهِ وَسَلِّمْ
تَسْلِيمًا وَارْزُقْنِي بِهِ مِنْ أَرْزَاقِكَ ٱلْحِسِّيَّةِ وَٱلْمَعْنَوِيَّةِ
رِزْقًا وَاسِعًا

Allāhumma yā Allāh yā Razzāq ṣalli ʿalā ʿabdika wa ḥabībika sayyidinā Muḥammad al-nabiyy wāsiṭat il-arzāq wa ʿalā ālihi wa ṣaḥbihi wa sallim taslīman war-zuqnī bihi min arzāqika il-ḥissiyyati wal-maʾnawiyyati rizqan wāsiʿā

O Allah, O Provider, send prayers and abundant Peace upon Your slave and beloved, our master, Muhammad, the Prophet who is the intermediary of provisions, and upon his family and companions, and provide for us, through him, from Your material and spiritual provisions, abundantly

ٱللَّهُمَّ يَا ٱللهُ يَا فَتَّاحُ صَلِّ عَلَىٰ عَبْدِكَ وَحَبِيبِكَ
سَيِّدِنَا مُحَمَّدٍ ٱلنَّبِيِّ جَامِعِ ٱلْفَتْحِ وَعَلَىٰ آلِهِ وَصَحْبِهِ
وَسَلِّمْ تَسْلِيمًا وَافْتَحْ لِي بِهِ فَتْحًا مُبِينًا

Allāhumma yā Allāh yā Fattāḥ ṣalli ʿalā ʿabdika wa ḥabībika sayyidinā Muḥammad al-nabiyy jāmiʾ il-fat'ḥ wa ʿalā ālihi wa ṣaḥbihi wa sallim taslīman waftaḥ lī bihi fat'ḥan mubīnā

O Allah, O Opener, send prayers and abundant Peace upon Your slave and beloved, our master, Muhammad, who is the combiner of the opening, and on his family and companions, and through him, grant me a clear opening

ٱللَّهُمَّ يَا ٱللَّهُ يَا عَلِيمُ صَلِّ عَلَىٰ عَبْدِكَ وَحَبِيبِكَ
سَيِّدِنَا مُحَمَّدٍ ٱلنَّبِيِّ ٱلعَلِيمِ وَعَلَىٰ آلِهِ وَصَحْبِهِ وَسَلِّمْ
تَسْلِيمًا وَعَلِّمْنِي بِهِ مِنْ لَدُنْكَ عِلْمًا

Allāhumma yā Allāh yā ʿAlīm ṣalli ʿalā ʿabdika wa ḥabībika sayyidinā Muḥammad al-nabiyy al-ʿalīm wa ʿalā ālihi wa ṣaḥbihi wa sallim taslīman wa ʿallimnī bihi min ladunka ʿilmā.

O Allah, O Omniscient One, send prayers and abundant Peace upon Your slave and beloved, our master, Muhammad, the knowledgeable Prophet, and upon his family and companions, and through him, teach me, from Yourself, knowledge

ٱللَّهُمَّ يَا ٱللهُ يَا بَاسِطُ صَلِّ عَلَىٰ عَبْدِكَ وَحَبِيبِكَ
سَيِّدِنَا مُحَمَّدٍ ٱلنَّبِيِّ بَاسِطِ ٱلْمَعْرُوفِ وَعَلَىٰ آلِهِ وَصَحْبِهِ
وَسَلِّمْ تَسْلِيمًا وَابْسُطْ لِي بِهِ بِسَاطَ كَرَمِكَ فَضْلًا
وَإِحْسَانًا

Allāhumma yā Allāh yā Bāsiṭ ṣalli ʿalā ʿabdika wa ḥabībika sayyidinā Muḥammad al-nabiyy bāsiṭi al-maʿrūf wa ʿalā ālihi wa ṣaḥbihi wa sallim taslīman wabsuṭ lī bihi bisāṭa karamika faḍlan wa iḥsānā

O Allah, O Extender, send prayers and abundant Peace upon Your slave and beloved, our master, Muhammad, who is the extender of goodness, and upon his family and companions, and through him, extend towards me Your generous extensions with favor and beneficence

ٱللَّٰهُمَّ يَا ٱللهُ يَا رَافِعُ صَلِّ عَلَىٰ عَبْدِكَ وَحَبِيبِكَ
سَيِّدِنَا مُحَمَّدٍ ٱلنَّبِيِّ ٱلرَّافِعِ وَعَلَىٰ آلِهِ وَصَحْبِهِ وَسَلِّمْ
تَسْلِيمًا وَارْفَعْنِي بِهِ إِلَىٰ مَرَاتِبِ قُرْبِكَ رِفْعًا

Allāhumma yā Allāh yā Rāfiʿ ṣalli ʿalā ʿabdika wa ḥabībika sayyidinā Muḥammad al-nabiyy al-rāfiʿ wa ʿalā ālihi wa ṣaḥbihi wa sallim taslīman warfaʿnī bihi ilā marātibi qurbika rifʿā

O Allah, O Elevator, send prayers and abundant Peace upon Your slave and beloved, our master, Muhammad, the elevated Prophet, and upon his family and companions, and through him, totally elevate me to the levels of Your proximity

ٱللَّهُمَّ يَا ٱللَّهُ يَا مُعِزُّ صَلِّ عَلَىٰ عَبْدِكَ وَحَبِيبِكَ سَيِّدِنَا
مُحَمَّدٍ ٱلنَّبِيِّ ٱلَّذِي تُعِزُّ مَنْ وَالَاهُ وَعَلَىٰ آلِهِ وَصَحْبِهِ
وَسَلِّمْ تَسْلِيمًا وَأَعِزَّنِي بِهِ فِي ٱلدَّارَيْنِ إِعْزَازًا

Allāhumma yā Allāh yā Mu'izz ṣalli 'alā 'abdika wa ḥabībika sayyidinā Muḥammad al-nabiyy al-ladhī tu'izzu man wālāhu wa 'alā ālihi wa ṣaḥbihi wa sallim taslīman wa a'izzanī bihi fil-dārayn i'zāzā

O Allah, O Honourer, send prayers and abundant Peace upon Your slave and beloved, our master, Muhammad, the Prophet that whomsoever draws near to him, is honoured by You, and upon his family and companions, and through him, greatly honor me in the two abodes

ٱللَّهُمَّ يَا ٱللهُ يَا سَمِيعُ صَلِّ عَلَىٰ عَبْدِكَ وَحَبِيبِكَ
سَيِّدِنَا مُحَمَّدٍ ٱلنَّبِيِّ ٱلسَّمِيعِ وَعَلَىٰ آلِهِ وَصَحْبِهِ وَسَلِّمْ
تَسْلِيمًا وَاسْمَعْنِي بِهِ وَاسْمَعْنِي مِنْكَ بِهِ إِسْمَاعًا

Allāhumma yā Allāh yā Samīʿ ṣalli ʿalā ʿabdika wa ḥabībika sayyidinā Muḥammad al-nabiyy al-samīʿ wa ʿalā ālihi wa ṣaḥbihi wa sallim taslīman wasmaʿnī bihi wasmaʿnī minka bihi ismāʿā

O Allah, O All-Hearing, send prayers and abundant Peace upon Your slave and beloved, our master, Muhammad, the Prophet of strong hearing, and upon his family and companions, and through him, entirely enable my hearing and my hearing of You

ٱللَّٰهُمَّ يَا ٱللهُ يَا بَصِيرُ صَلِّ عَلَىٰ عَبْدِكَ وَحَبِيبِكَ
سَيِّدِنَا مُحَمَّدٍ ٱلنَّبِيِّ ٱلبَصِيرِ وَعَلَىٰ آلِهِ وَصَحْبِهِ وَسَلِّمْ
تَسْلِيمًا وَبِهِ بَصِّرْنِي بِكَ تَبْصِيرًا

Allāhumma yā Allāh yā Baṣīr ṣalli ʿalā ʿabdika wa ḥabībika sayyidinā Muḥammad al-nabiyy al-baṣīr wa ʿalā ālihi wa ṣaḥbihi wa sallim taslīman wa bihi baṣṣirnī bika tabṣīrā

O Allah, O All-Seeing, send prayers and abundant Peace upon Your slave and beloved, our master, Muhammad, the Prophet of strong sight, and upon his family and companions, and through him, enormously grant me insight into You

اَللّٰهُمَّ يَا اَللّٰهُ يَا حَكَمُ صَلِّ عَلَىٰ عَبْدِكَ وَحَبِيبِكَ
سَيِّدِنَا مُحَمَّدٍ ٱلنَّبِيِّ ٱلْحَاكِمِ بِٱلْحَقِّ وَٱلْعَدْلِ
وَٱلْهُدَىٰ وَعَلَىٰ آلِهِ وَصَحْبِهِ وَسَلِّمْ تَسْلِيمًا وَارْزُقْنِي بِهِ
ٱلْاِسْتِسْلَامَ لِحُكْمِكَ وَٱلْعَمَلَ عَلَىٰ أَحْكَامِ شَرْعِكَ
وَاحْكُمْ لِي بِٱلْفَوْزِ يَوْمَ ٱللِّقَاءِ يَا أَحْكَمَ ٱلْحَاكِمِينَ

Allāhumma yā Allāh yā Ḥakam ṣalli ʿalā ʿabdika wa ḥabībika sayyidinā Muḥammad al-nabiyy al-ḥākim bil-ḥaqq wal-ʾadl wal-hudā wa ʿalā ālihi wa ṣaḥbihi wa sallim taslīman war-zuqnī bihi al-istislāma li-ḥukmika wal-ʾamala ʿalā aḥkāmi sharʾika waḥ-kum lī bil-fawzi yawma al-liqāi yā Aḥkam al-hākimīn

O Allah, O Giver of justice, send prayers and abundant Peace upon Your slave and beloved, our master, Muhammad, the authoritative Prophet with truth, fairness and guidance, and upon his family and companions, and through him, endow me with submission to Your Ruling, implementation of Your Legal Rulings and decree for me success on the Day of Judgment, O Most Just Giver of justice

ٱللّٰهُمَّ يَا ٱللهُ يَا لَطِيفُ صَلِّ عَلَىٰ عَبْدِكَ وَحَبِيبِكَ
سَيِّدِنَا مُحَمَّدٍ ٱلنَّبِيِّ ٱللَّطِيفِ وَعَلَىٰ آلِهِ وَصَحْبِهِ وَسَلِّمْ
تَسْلِيمًا وَاجْرِ بِهِ يَا رَبِّ لُطْفَكَ ٱلْخَفِيَّ فِي أُمُورِي
وَأُمُورِ ٱلْمُسْلِمِينَ

Allāhumma yā Allāh yā Laṭīf ṣalli ʿalā ʿabdika wa ḥabībika sayyidinā Muḥammad al-nabiyy al-laṭīf wa ʿalā ālihi wa ṣaḥbihi wa sallim taslīman wajri bihi yā rabbi lutfak al-khafiyy fī umūrī wa umūr il-muslimīn

O Allah, O Most Gentle, send prayers and abundant Peace upon Your slave and beloved, our master, Muhammad, the gentle Prophet, and upon his family and companions, and through him, O Lord, let Your subtle gentleness permeate my affairs and the affairs of the Muslims

ٱللَّهُمَّ يَا ٱللهُ يَا خَبِيرُ صَلِّ عَلَىٰ عَبْدِكَ وَحَبِيبِكَ
سَيِّدِنَا مُحَمَّدٍ ٱلنَّبِيِّ ٱلْخَبِيرِ وَعَلَىٰ آلِهِ وَصَحْبِهِ وَسَلِّمْ
تَسْلِيمًا وَاجْعَلْنِي بِأَسْرَارِ مَا أَوْحَيْتَهُ إِلَيْهِ خَبِيرًا

Allāhumma yā Allāh yā Khabīr ṣalli ʿalā ʿabdika wa ḥabībika sayyidinā Muḥammad al-nabiyy al-khabīr wa ʿalā ālihi wa ṣaḥbihi wa sallim taslīman wajʿalnī bi-asrāri mā awḥaytahu ilayhi khabīrā

O Allah, O All-Aware, send prayers and abundant Peace upon Your slave and beloved, our master, Muhammad, the all-aware Prophet, and upon his family and companions, and through him, make me aware of the secrets You revealed to him

ٱللَّهُمَّ يَا ٱللهُ يَا حَلِيمُ صَلِّ عَلَىٰ عَبْدِكَ وَحَبِيبِكَ
سَيِّدِنَا مُحَمَّدٍ ٱلنَّبِيِّ ٱلْحَلِيمِ وَعَلَىٰ آلِهِ وَصَحْبِهِ وَسَلِّمْ
تَسْلِيمًا وَارْزُقْنِي بِهِ حِلْمًا وَعِلْمًا وَإِيمَانًا وَيَقِينًا

Allāhumma yā Allāh yā Ḥalīm ṣalli 'alā 'abdika wa ḥabībika sayyidinā Muḥammad al-nabiyy al-ḥalīm wa 'alā ālihi wa ṣaḥbihi wa sallim taslīman warzuqnī bihi ḥilman wa 'ilman wa īmānan wa yaqīnā

O Allah, O Most Forbearing, send prayers and abundant Peace upon Your slave and beloved, our master, Muhammad, the forbearing Prophet, and upon his family and companions, and through him, endow me with forbearance, knowledge, faith and certainty

ٱللَّهُمَّ يَا ٱللهُ يَا حَفِيظُ صَلِّ عَلَىٰ عَبْدِكَ وَحَبِيبِكَ
سَيِّدِنَا مُحَمَّدٍ ٱلنَّبِيِّ ٱلْحَفِيظِ وَعَلَىٰ آلِهِ وَصَحْبِهِ وَسَلِّمْ
تَسْلِيمًا وَاجْعَلْنِي مُسْتَوْدِعًا لِأَسْرَارِ ٱلْمَعْرِفَةِ
وَٱلْمَحَبَّةِ حَفِيظًا وَكُنْ لِي مِنْ جَمِيعِ ٱلْأَسْوَاءِ
فِي ٱلدَّارَيْنِ حَافِظًا

Allāhumma yā Allāh yā Ḥafīẓ ṣalli ʿalā ʿabdika wa ḥabībika sayyidinā Muḥammad al-nabiyy al-ḥafīẓ wa ʿalā ālihi wa ṣaḥbihi wa sallim taslīman waj'alnī mustawdi'an li-asrāri al-ma'rifah wa al-maḥabbah ḥafīẓan wa kun lī min jamī' al-aswāi fil-dārayn ḥāfiẓā

O Allah, O All-Protecting, send prayers and abundant Peace upon Your slave and beloved, our master, Muhammad, the Protected Prophet, and upon his family and companions, and through him, make me a protected depository of secrets of knowledge and love, and be my protector in the two abodes from all evil

ٱللّٰهُمَّ يَا ٱللهُ يَا جَلِيلُ صَلِّ عَلَىٰ عَبْدِكَ وَحَبِيبِكَ
سَيِّدِنَا مُحَمَّدٍ ٱلنَّبِيِّ ٱلْجَلِيلِ وَعَلَىٰ آلِهِ وَصَحْبِهِ وَسَلِّمْ
تَسْلِيمًا وَجَلِّلْنِي بِأَنْوَارِ قُرْبِكَ وَاجْعَلْ لِي عِنْدَكَ
مَقَامًا جَلِيلًا

Allāhumma yā Allāh yā Jalīl ṣalli ʿalā ʿabdika wa ḥabībika sayyidinā Muḥammad al-nabiyy al-jalīl wa ʿalā ālihi wa ṣaḥbihi wa sallim taslīman wa jallilnī bi-anwāri qurbika wajʿal lī ʿindaka maqāman jalīla

O Allah, O Majestic One, send prayers and abundant Peace upon Your slave and beloved, our master, Muhammad, the majestic Prophet, and upon his family and companions, and through him, reveal to me the lights of Your proximity and appoint for me a majestic rank in Your presence

ٱللّٰهُمَّ يَا ٱللّٰهُ يَا كَرِيمُ صَلِّ عَلَىٰ عَبْدِكَ وَحَبِيبِكَ سَيِّدِنَا مُحَمَّدٍ ٱلنَّبِيِّ ٱلْكَرِيمِ وَعَلَىٰ آلِهِ وَصَحْبِهِ وَسَلِّمْ تَسْلِيمًا وَكَرِّمْنِي بِهِ تَكْرِيمًا

Allāhumma yā Allāh yā Karīm ṣalli ʿalā ʿabdika wa ḥabībika sayyidinā Muḥammad al-nabiyy al-karīm wa ʿalā ālihi wa ṣaḥbihi wa sallim taslīman wa karrimnī bihi takrīmā

O Allah, O Kind One, send prayers and abundant Peace upon Your slave and beloved, our master, Muhammad, the kind Prophet, and upon his family and companions, and through him, vastly show me kindness

NUMBER TWENTY-SEVEN

ٱللَّهُمَّ يَا ٱللَّهُ يَا مُجِيبُ صَلِّ عَلَىٰ عَبْدِكَ وَحَبِيبِكَ
سَيِّدِنَا مُحَمَّدٍ ٱلنَّبِيِّ ٱلْمُجِيبِ وَعَلَىٰ آلِهِ وَصَحْبِهِ وَسَلِّمْ
تَسْلِيمًا وَكُنْ لِدُعَائِنَا بِهِ مُجِيبًا وَاجْعَلْنِي لِنِدَائِكَ
وَنِدَائِهِ مُلَبِّيًا مُسْتَجِيبًا

Allāhumma yā Allāh yā Mujīb ṣalli ʿalā ʿabdika wa ḥabībika sayyidinā Muḥammad al-nabiyy al-mujīb wa ʿalā ālihi wa ṣaḥbihi wa sallim taslīman wa kun li-duʿāinā bihi mujīban wajʿalnī li-nidāika wa nidāihi mulabbiyan mustajība

O Allah, O Responsive One, send prayers and abundant Peace upon Your slave and beloved, our master, Muhammad, the responsive Prophet, and upon his family and companions, and through him, answer our supplications and make me highly responsive to Your call, and his call

ٱللَّٰهُمَّ يَا ٱللَّٰهُ يَا وَاسِعُ صَلِّ عَلَىٰ عَبْدِكَ وَحَبِيبِكَ سَيِّدِنَا
مُحَمَّدٍ ٱلنَّبِيِّ ٱلْوَاسِعِ وَعَلَىٰ آلِهِ وَصَحْبِهِ وَسَلِّمْ تَسْلِيمًا
وَوَسِّعْ لِي بِهِ فِي ٱلْعِلْمِ وَٱلْفَهْمِ وَٱلْمَعْرِفَةِ وَٱلْمَحَبَّةِ
وَٱلْمَشْهَدِ وَٱلْأَرْزَاقِ وَٱلْإِنْتِفَاعِ وَٱلنَّفْعِ وَهَبْ لِي مِنْ
لَدُنْكَ عَطَاءً وَاسِعًا

Allāhumma yā Allāh yā Wāsi' ṣalli 'alā 'abdika wa ḥabībika sayyidinā Muḥammad al-nabiyy al-wāsi' wa 'alā ālihi wa ṣaḥbihi wa sallim taslīman wa wassi' lī bihi fil-'ilm wa al-fahmi wa al-ma'rifati wa al-maḥabbati wa al-mash'hadi wa al-arzāqi wa al-intifā' wa an-nafi' wa hab lī min ladunka 'aṭā'an wāsi'an

O Allah, O All-Encompassing, send prayers and abundant Peace upon Your slave and beloved, our master, Muhammad, the all-encompassing Prophet, and upon his family and companions, and through him, expand me in knowledge, understanding, gnosis, love, view, provisions, giving benefit and receiving benefit, and grant me, from Thyself, a great portion

ٱللَّهُمَّ يَا ٱللهُ يَا وَاسِعُ صَلِّ عَلَىٰ عَبْدِكَ وَحَبِيبِكَ
سَيِّدِنَا مُحَمَّدٍ ٱلنَّبِيِّ ٱلْوَاسِعِ وَعَلَىٰ آلِهِ وَصَحْبِهِ وَسَلِّمْ
تَسْلِيمًا وَاجْعَلْنِي بِهِ عَبْدًا وَاسِعَ ٱلْمَشَاهِدِ وَٱلْعَطَايَا
وَٱلْمَحَامِدِ وَٱلْمَزَايَا يَا أَكْرَمَ ٱلْأَكْرَمِينَ

Allāhumma yā Allāh yā Wāsiʿ ṣalli ʿalā ʿabdika wa ḥabībika sayyidinā Muḥammad al-nabiyy al-wāsiʿ wa ʿalā ālihi wa ṣaḥbihi wa sallim taslīman wajʿalnī bihi ʿabdan wāsiʿ al-mashāhidi wa al-ʿaṭāyā wa al-maḥāmidi wa al-mazāyā yā Akram al-akramīn

O Allah, O All-Encompassing, send prayers and abundant Peace upon Your slave and beloved, our master, Muhammad, the all-encompassing Prophet, and upon his family and companions, and through him, make me a slave possessing vast views, gifts, praiseworthy acts and virtues, O Most Generous of the generous

ٱللّٰهُمَّ يَا ٱللهُ يَا حَكِيمُ صَلِّ عَلَىٰ عَبْدِكَ وَحَبِيبِكَ
سَيِّدِنَا مُحَمَّدٍ ٱلنَّبِيِّ ٱلْحَكِيمِ وَعَلَىٰ آلِهِ وَصَحْبِهِ وَسَلِّمْ
تَسْلِيمًا وَآتِنِي بِهِ ٱلْحِكْمَةَ وَخَيْرًا كَثِيرًا

Allāhumma yā Allāh yā Hakīm ṣalli ʿalā ʿabdika wa ḥabībika sayyidinā Muḥammad al-nabiyy al-ḥakīm wa ʿalā ālihi wa ṣaḥbihi wa sallim taslīman wa ātinī bihi al-ḥikmah wa khayran kathīrā

O Allah, O All-Wise, send prayers and abundant Peace upon Your slave and beloved, our master, Muhammad, the wise Prophet, and upon his family and companions, and through him, grant me wisdom and great goodness

NUMBER THIRTY-ONE

ٱللَّهُمَّ يَا ٱللهُ يَا وَدُودُ صَلِّ عَلَىٰ عَبْدِكَ وَحَبِيبِكَ
سَيِّدِنَا مُحَمَّدٍ ٱلنَّبِيِّ ٱلْوَدُودِ وَعَلَىٰ آلِهِ وَصَحْبِهِ وَسَلِّمْ
تَسْلِيمًا وَأَذِقْنِي بِهِ لَذَّةَ وِدَادِكَ وَاجْعَلْ لِي فِي قُلُوبِ
أَوْلِيَائِكَ مَوَدَّةً أَكِيدَةً

Allāhumma yā Allāh yā Wadūd ṣalli ʿalā ʿabdika wa ḥabībika sayyidinā Muḥammad al-nabiyy al-wadūd wa ʿalā ālihi wa ṣaḥbihi wa sallim taslīman wa adhiqnī bihi ladhdhata widādika wa-ijʿal lī fī qulūbi awliyāika mawaddata akīdah

O Allah, O Most Loving, send prayers and abundant Peace upon Your slave and beloved, our master, Muhammad, the most loving Prophet, and upon his family and companions, and through him, allow me to taste the sweetness of loving You and make me dearly beloved in the hearts of Your close friends

ٱللَّهُمَّ يَا ٱللهُ يَا مَجِيدُ صَلِّ عَلَىٰ عَبْدِكَ وَحَبِيبِكَ
سَيِّدِنَا مُحَمَّدٍ ٱلنَّبِيِّ ٱلْمَجِيدِ وَعَلَىٰ آلِهِ وَصَحْبِهِ وَسَلِّمْ
تَسْلِيمًا وَاجْعَلْ لِي بِحَقِيقَةِ ٱلتَّوْحِيدِ وَتَحْقِيقِ
ٱلْعُبُودِيَّةِ ٱلْمَحْضَةِ ٱلْخَالِصَةِ لَكَ مَجْدًا أَكِيدًا

Allāhumma yā Allāh yā Majīd ṣalli ʿalā ʿabdika wa ḥabībika sayyidinā Muḥammad al-nabiyy al-majīd wa ʿalā ālihi wa ṣaḥbihi wa sallim taslīman wa-ijʿal lī bi-haqīqati al-tawḥīdi wa taḥqīqi al-ʾubūdiyyah al-maḥḍati al-khāliṣati laka majdan akīda

O Allah, O Glorious One, send prayers and abundant Peace upon Your slave and beloved, our master, Muhammad, the glorious Prophet, and upon his family and companions, and through him, through the reality of monotheism and the realization of fortified pure worship, make me greatly glorified

ٱللّٰهُمَّ يَا ٱللّٰهُ يَا بَاعِثُ صَلِّ عَلَىٰ عَبْدِكَ وَحَبِيبِكَ
سَيِّدِنَا مُحَمَّدٍ ٱلنَّبِيِّ ٱلْمَبْعُوثِ مِنْكَ بِٱلرَّحْمَةِ وَعَلَىٰ آلِهِ
وَصَحْبِهِ وَسَلِّمْ تَسْلِيمًا وَاجْعَلْنِي لَهُ يَوْمَ ٱلْبَعْثِ رَفِيقًا

Allāhumma yā Allāh yā Bā'ith ṣalli 'alā 'abdika wa ḥabībika sayyidinā Muḥammad al-nabiyy al-mab'ūthi minka bi al-rahmati wa 'alā ālihi wa ṣaḥbihi wa sallim taslīman waj'alnī la-hū yawm al-ba'thi rafīqā

O Allah, O You who resurrects, send prayers and abundant Peace upon Your slave and beloved, our master, Muhammad, the Prophet sent by you with mercy, and upon his family and companions, and through him, make me his friend on the Day of Resurrection

ٱللّٰهُمَّ يَا ٱللهُ يَا شَهِيدُ صَلِّ عَلَىٰ عَبْدِكَ وَحَبِيبِكَ
سَيِّدِنَا مُحَمَّدٍ ٱلنَّبِيِّ ٱلشَّهِيدِ وَعَلَىٰ آلِهِ وَصَحْبِهِ وَسَلِّمْ
تَسْلِيمًا وَارْزُقْنِي بِهِ كَمَالَ ٱلشُّهُودِ وَتَوَفَّنِي شَهِيدًا
وَأَشْهِدْنِي بِهِ عَجَائِبَ وَاسِعَاتِ كَرَمِكَ وَانْصُرْنِي بِهِ
فِي ٱلْحَيَاةِ ٱلدُّنْيَا وَيَوْمَ يَقُومُ ٱلْأَشْهَادُ

Allāhumma yā Allāh yā Shahīd ṣalli ʿalā ʿabdika wa ḥabībika sayyidinā Muḥammad al-nabiyy al-shahīd wa ʿalā ālihi wa ṣaḥbihi wa sallim taslīman warzuqnī bihi kamāl al-shuhūd wa tawaffanī shahīdan wa ash'hidnī bihi ʿajāʾib wāsiʿāti karamika wansurnī bihi fil-hayāt al-dunyā wa yawma yaqūm al-ashhād

O Allah, O Witness, send prayers and abundant Peace upon Your slave and beloved, our master, Muhammad, the witnessing Prophet, and upon his family and companions, and through him, and grant me complete witnessing and martyrdom, and through him, make me witness Your amazingly vast generosity, and through him, grant me victory in this life and on the Day of Judgment

NUMBER THIRTY-FIVE

اَللّٰهُمَّ يَا اَللّٰهُ يَا حَقُّ صَلِّ عَلَىٰ عَبْدِكَ وَحَبِيبِكَ سَيِّدِنَا
مُحَمَّدٍ ٱلنَّبِيِّ ٱلْحَقِّ وَعَلَىٰ آلِهِ وَصَحْبِهِ وَسَلِّمْ تَسْلِيمًا
وَحَقِّقْنِي بِحَقَائِقِ ٱلْحَقِّ تَحْقِيقًا

Allāhumma yā Allāh yā Ḥaqq ṣalli 'alā 'abdika wa ḥabībika sayyidinā Muḥammad al-nabiyy al-ḥaqq wa 'alā ālihi wa ṣaḥbihi wa sallim taslīman wa ḥaqqiqnī bi-ḥaqāiq al-haqq tahqīqā

O Allah, O Absolute Truth, send prayers and abundant Peace upon Your slave and beloved, our master, Muhammad, the Prophet of truth, and upon his family and companions, and through him, firmly establish within me the realities of truth

ٱللَّٰهُمَّ يَا ٱللَّٰهُ يَا قَوِيُّ صَلِّ عَلَىٰ عَبْدِكَ وَحَبِيبِكَ
سَيِّدِنَا مُحَمَّدٍ ٱلنَّبِيِّ ٱلْقَوِيِّ بِكَ وَعَلَىٰ آلِهِ وَصَحْبِهِ
وَسَلِّمْ تَسْلِيمًا وَقَوِّ لِي بِهِ ٱلْإِيمَانَ وَٱلْيَقِينَ وَأَمِدَّنِي
بِقُوَّةٍ مِنْ قُوَّتِكَ فِي جَمِيعِ قُوَايَ ٱلظَّاهِرَةِ وَالْبَاطِنَةِ فِي
كُلِّ شَأْنٍ وَحِينٍ وَارْحَمْ بِهِ ضَعْفِي وَكُنْ لِي مُعِينًا

Allāhumma yā Allāh yā Qawī ṣalli ʿalā ʿabdika wa ḥabībika sayyidinā Muḥammad al-nabiyy al-qawī bi-ka wa ʿalā ālihi wa ṣaḥbihi wa sallim taslīman wa qawwi lī bihi al-īmān wa al-yaqīn wa amiddanī biquwwatika fī jamīʾ quwāya al-ẓāhirah wa al-bāṭinah fī kulli shaʾnin wa hīn warḥam bihi ḍaʿfī wa kun lī muʾīnā

O Allah, O All-Strong, send prayers and abundant Peace upon Your slave and beloved, our master, Muhammad, the Prophet of strength by You, and upon his family and companions, and through him, strengthen my faith and certainty, assist me by Your strength in all my outward and inward strengths, in everything and every time, and through him, show mercy upon me for my weakness and be of assistance to me

ٱللّٰهُمَّ يَا ٱللّٰهُ يَا مَتِينُ صَلِّ عَلَىٰ عَبْدِكَ وَحَبِيبِكَ
سَيِّدِنَا مُحَمَّدٍ ٱلنَّبِيِّ صَاحِبِ ٱلدِّينِ ٱلْمَتِينِ وَعَلَىٰ آلِهِ
وَصَحْبِهِ وَسَلِّمْ تَسْلِيمًا وَارْزُقْنِي ٱلْاِعْتِصَامَ بِٱلْحَبْلِ
ٱلْمَتِينِ وَاجْعَلْ لِي فِي وُصْلَتِكَ وَوُصْلَتِهِ حَبْلًا مَتِينًا

Allāhumma yā Allāh yā Matīn ṣalli ʿalā ʿabdika wa ḥabībika sayyidinā Muḥammad al-nabiyy ṣāhib al-dīn al-matīn wa ʿalā ālihi wa ṣaḥbihi wa sallim taslīman wa-urzuqnī al-iʿtiṣām bi-al-ḥabl al-matīn wa-ijʿal lī fī wuṣlatika wa wuṣlatihi ḥablan matīnā

O Allah, O Steadfast One, send prayers and abundant Peace upon Your slave and beloved, our master, Muhammad, the Prophet of the steadfast religion, and upon his family and companions, and endow me with a firm holding of the steadfast rope, and make for me a steadfast rope for Your connection and his connection

ٱللَّٰهُمَّ يَا ٱللَّٰهُ يَا وَلِيُّ صَلِّ عَلَىٰ عَبْدِكَ وَحَبِيبِكَ سَيِّدِنَا
مُحَمَّدٍ ٱلنَّبِيِّ ٱلْوَلِيِّ وَعَلَىٰ آلِهِ وَصَحْبِهِ وَسَلِّمْ تَسْلِيمًا
وَكُنْ لِي بِهِ وَلِيًّا نَصِيرًا

Allāhumma yā Allāh yā Waliyy ṣalli ʿalā ʿabdika wa ḥabībika sayyidinā Muḥammad al-nabiyy al-waliyy wa ʿalā ālihi wa ṣaḥbihi wa sallim taslīman wa kun lī bihi waliyyan naṣīrā

O Allah, O Supporter, send prayers and abundant Peace upon Your slave and beloved, our master, Muhammad, the supported Prophet, and upon his family and companions, and through him, be my helpful supporter

NUMBER THIRTY-NINE

ٱللَّهُمَّ يَا ٱللهُ يَا حَمِيدُ صَلِّ عَلَىٰ عَبْدِكَ وَحَبِيبِكَ
سَيِّدِنَا مُحَمَّدٍ ٱلنَّبِيِّ ٱلْحَمِيدِ وَعَلَىٰ آلِهِ وَصَحْبِهِ وَسَلِّمْ
تَسْلِيمًا وَارْفَعْنِي بِهِ إِلَىٰ مَرَاتِبِ ٱلْحَمَّادِينَ لَكَ
ٱلْمُتَحَقِّقِينَ بِحَمْدِكَ وَاجْعَلْ لِي بِهِ عَيْشًا حَمِيدًا
وَاجْعَلْنِي فِي ٱلدَّارَيْنِ عَبْدًا مَحْمُودًا

Allāhumma yā Ḥamīd ṣalli ʿalā ʿabdika wa ḥabībika sayyidinā Muḥammad al-nabiyy al-ḥamīd wa ʿalā ālihi wa ṣaḥbihi wa sallim taslīman warfaʿnī bihi ilā marātib al-ḥammādīn laka al-mutaḥaqqiqīna bi-ḥamdika wajʿal lī bihi ʿayshan ḥamīdan wa-ijʿalnī fī al-dārayni ʿabdan maḥmūdā

O Allah, O Praiseworthy, send prayers and abundant Peace upon Your slave and beloved, our master, Muhammad, the praiseworthy Prophet, and upon his family and companions, and through him, elevate me to the ranks of those who abundantly praise You and are established in Your praise, and through him, make me live a praiseworthy life and make me a praiseworthy slave in the two abodes

ٱللَّٰهُمَّ يَا ٱللَّٰهُ يَا مُبْدِئُ صَلِّ عَلَىٰ عَبْدِكَ وَحَبِيبِكَ
سَيِّدِنَا مُحَمَّدٍ ٱلنَّبِيِّ ٱلَّذِي ٱبْتَدَأْتَ بِنُورِهِ ٱلْوُجُودِ
وَعَلَىٰ آلِهِ وَصَحْبِهِ وَسَلِّمْ تَسْلِيمًا وَاعْطِنَا بِهِ مَا
سَأَلْنَاكَ وَابْتَدِئْنَا بِمَا لَمْ نَسْأَلْكَ مِنْ وَاسِعِ ٱلْجُودِ
فَضْلًا وَإِحْسَانًا

Allāhumma yā Allāh yā Mubdi ṣalli ʿalā ʿabdika wa ḥabībika sayyidinā Muḥammad al-nabiyy al-ladhī ibtadaʾta bi-nūrihi al-wujūd wa ʿalā ālihi wa ṣaḥbihi wa sallim taslīman waʿṭinā bihi mā saʾalnāka wabtadiʾnā bi-mā lam nasʾalka min wāsiʿ al-jūdi faḍlan wa iḥsānā

O Allah, O Initiator, send prayers and abundant Peace upon Your slave and beloved, our master, Muhammad, the Prophet by who's light You initiated existence, and upon his family and companions, and through him, grant us that which we have asked You and initiate for us that which we have not asked You, out of Your vast Generosity with favor and beneficence

ٱللَّٰهُمَّ يَا ٱللَّٰهُ يَا مُعِيدُ صَلِّ عَلَىٰ عَبْدِكَ وَحَبِيبِكَ
سَيِّدِنَا مُحَمَّدٍ ٱلنَّبِيِّ شَفِيعِي فِي ٱلْمَعَادِ وَعَلَىٰ آلِهِ
وَصَحْبِهِ وَسَلِّمْ تَسْلِيمًا وَأَعِدْ عَلَيْنَا بِهِ عَوَائِدَ ٱلْخَيْرِ
ظَاهِرًا وَبَاطِنًا

Allāhumma yā Allāh yā Mu'īd ṣalli 'alā 'abdika wa ḥabībika sayyidinā Muḥammad al-nabiyy shafī'ī fil-ma'ādi wa 'alā ālihi wa ṣaḥbihi wa sallim taslīman wa a'id 'alaynā bihi 'awā'id al-khayr ẓāhiran wa bāṭinā.

O Allah, O Restorer, send prayers and abundant Peace upon Your slave and beloved, our master, Muhammad, the Prophet who is my intercessor on the Day of Judgment, and upon his family and companions, and through him, restore within us practices of goodness, outwardly and inwardly

ٱللّٰهُمَّ يَا ٱللهُ يَا مُحْيِي صَلِّ عَلَىٰ عَبْدِكَ وَحَبِيبِكَ
سَيِّدِنَا مُحَمَّدٍ ٱلنَّبِيِّ مُحْيِي ٱلْهُدَىٰ فِي ٱلْقُلُوبِ وَعَلَىٰ
آلِهِ وَصَحْبِهِ وَسَلِّمْ تَسْلِيمًا وأَحْيِ بِهِ قَلْبِي وَأَحْيِنِي بِهِ
حَيَاةً طَيِّبَةً وَأَحْيِ فِينَا وَبِنَا سُنَّتَهُ

Allāhumma yā Allāh yā Muḥyī ṣalli ʿalā ʿabdika wa ḥabībika sayyidinā Muḥammad al-nabiyy muḥyī al-hudā fī al-qulūb wa ʿalā ālihi wa ṣaḥbihi wa sallim taslīman wa aḥyi bihi qalbī wa ahyinī bihi ḥayātan ṭayyibatan wa aḥyi fīnā wa binā sunnatah

O Allah, O Giver of life, send prayers and abundant Peace upon Your slave and beloved, our master, Muhammad, the Prophet who gives life to the heart's guidance, and upon his family and companions, and through him, bring life to my heart, and through him, make me live a good life and bring to life within us and through us, his lifestyle

NUMBER FORTY-THREE

ٱللَّهُمَّ يَا ٱللهُ يَا حَيُّ صَلِّ عَلَىٰ عَبْدِكَ وَحَبِيبِكَ سَيِّدِنَا
مُحَمَّدٍ ٱلنَّبِيِّ ٱلْحَيِّ وَعَلَىٰ آلِهِ وَصَحْبِهِ وَسَلِّمْ تَسْلِيمًا
وَاجْعَلْنَا بِهِ فِي أَحْيَاءٍ عِنْدَ رَبِّهِمْ يُرْزَقُونَ

Allāhumma yā Allāh yā Ḥayy ṣalli ʿalā ʿabdika wa ḥabībika sayyidinā Muḥammad al-nabiyy al-ḥayy wa ʿalā ālihi wa ṣaḥbihi wa sallim taslīman wajʿalnā bihi fī aḥyāʾin ʿinda rabbi-him yurzaqūn

O Allah, O Ever-Living, send prayers and abundant Peace upon Your slave and beloved, our master, Muhammad, the alive Prophet, and upon his family and companions, and through him, make us alive in Your company, receiving provision

ٱللَّهُمَّ يَا ٱللهُ يَا قَيُّومُ صَلِّ عَلَىٰ عَبْدِكَ وَحَبِيبِكَ سَيِّدِنَا
مُحَمَّدٍ ٱلنَّبِيِّ ٱلْقَائِمِ بِٱلْحَقِّ وَعَلَىٰ آلِهِ وَصَحْبِهِ وَسَلِّمْ
تَسْلِيمًا وقَوِّمْنِي عَلَىٰ صِرَاطِكَ ٱلْمُسْتَقِيمِ تَقْوِيمًا

Allāhumma yā Allāh yā Qayyūm ṣalli ʿalā ʿabdik wa ḥabībika sayyidinā Muḥammad al-nabiyy al-qāʾim bi-al-ḥaqqi wa ʿalā ālihi wa ṣaḥbihi wa sallim taslīman wa qawwimnī ʿalā ṣirāṭik al-mustaqīm taqwīmā

O Allah, O Sustainer, send prayers and abundant Peace upon Your slave and beloved, our master, Muhammad, the steadfast Prophet upon truth, and upon his family and companions, and through him, make me firmly steadfast upon Your straight path

ٱللّٰهُمَّ يَا ٱللّٰهُ يَا وَاجِدُ صَلِّ عَلَىٰ عَبْدِكَ وَحَبِيبِكَ
سَيِّدِنَا مُحَمَّدٍ ٱلنَّبِيِّ ٱلْوَاجِدِ وَعَلَىٰ آلِهِ وَصَحْبِهِ وَسَلِّمْ
تَسْلِيمًا وَهَبْ لِي بِهِ وَجْدًا أَجِدُ بِهِ هَزَّةَ ٱلشَّوْقِ إِلَىٰ
ٱللِّقَاءِ فِي لُطْفٍ وَعَافِيَةٍ

Allāhumma yā Allāh yā Wājid ṣalli ʿalā ʿabdika wa ḥabībika sayyidinā Muḥammad al-nabiyy al-wājid wa ʿalā ālihi wa ṣaḥbihi wa sallim taslīman wa hab lī bihi wajdan ajidu bihi hazzat al-shawqi ilā al-liqā fī luṭfin wa ʿāfiyah

O Allah, O Perceiver, send prayers and abundant Peace upon Your slave and beloved, our master, Muhammad, the Prophet of perception, and upon his family and companions, and through him, endow me with a strong emotion from which I find an agitated feeling of desire to meet You, with gentleness and wellbeing

ٱللّٰهُمَّ يَا ٱللهُ يَا مَاجِدُ صَلِّ عَلَىٰ عَبْدِكَ وَحَبِيبِكَ
سَيِّدِنَا مُحَمَّدٍ ٱلنَّبِيِّ ٱلْمَاجِدِ وَعَلَىٰ آلِهِ وَصَحْبِهِ وَسَلِّمْ
تَسْلِيمًا وَاجْعَلْنِي بِهِ فِي مَنَازِلِ قُرْبِكَ مَاجِدًا كَرِيمًا

Allāhumma yā Allāh yā Mājid ṣalli ʿalā ʿabdika wa ḥabībika sayyidinā Muḥammad al-nabiyy al-mājid wa ʿalā ālihi wa ṣaḥbihi wa sallim taslīman waj'alnī bihi fī manāzili qurbika mājidan karīmā

O Allah, O Magnificent One, send prayers and abundant Peace upon Your slave and beloved, our master, Muhammad, the magnificent Prophet, and upon his family and companions and through him, make me, in the levels of proximity to You, magnificent and honorable

اَللّٰهُمَّ يَا اَللّٰهُ يَا وَاحِدُ صَلِّ عَلَىٰ عَبْدِكَ وَحَبِيبِكَ
سَيِّدِنَا مُحَمَّدٍ ٱلنَّبِيِّ ٱلْوَاحِدِ وَعَلَىٰ آلِهِ وَصَحْبِهِ وَسَلِّمْ
تَسْلِيمًا وَاجْعَلْنِي بِهِ رَاسِخَ ٱلْقَدَمِ فِي حَقِيقَةِ ٱلتَّوْحِيدِ
مَنًّا مِنْكَ عَظِيمًا

Allāhumma yā Allāh yā Wāḥid ṣalli ʿalā ʿabdika wa ḥabībika sayyidinā Muḥammad al-nabiyy al-wāḥid wa ʿalā ālihi wa ṣaḥbihi wa sallim taslīman wajʿalnī bihi rāsikh al-qadami fī ḥaqīqat al-tawḥīd mannan minka ʿaẓīmā

O Allah, O Unique one, send prayers and abundant Peace upon Your slave and beloved, our master, Muhammad, the unique Prophet, and upon his family and companions, and through him, make me firmly grounded in the reality of monotheism by Your Grace, completely

ٱللّٰهُمَّ يَا ٱللهُ يَا أَحَدُ صَلِّ عَلَىٰ عَبْدِكَ وَحَبِيبِكَ
سَيِّدِنَا مُحَمَّدٍ ٱلنَّبِيِّ ٱلْأَحْمَدِ وَعَلَىٰ آلِهِ وَصَحْبِهِ وَسَلِّمْ
تَسْلِيمًا وأَشْهِدْنِي بِهِ سِرَّ ٱلْأَحَدِيَّةِ لَكَ إِشْهَادًا

Allāhumma yā Allāh yā Aḥad ṣalli ʿalā ʿabdika wa ḥabībika sayyidinā Muḥammad al-nabiyy al-aḥmad wa ʿalā ālihi wa ṣaḥbihi wa sallim taslīman wa ash'hidnī bihi sirra al-aḥadiyyah laka ishhādā

O Allah, O Indivisible One, send prayers and abundant Peace upon Your slave and beloved, our master, Muhammad, the indivisible Prophet, and upon his family and companions, and through him, cause us to totally witness the secret of Your Indivisibility

ٱللَّهُمَّ يَا ٱللهُ يَا فَرْدُ صَلِّ عَلَىٰ عَبْدِكَ وَحَبِيبِكَ سَيِّدِنَا
مُحَمَّدٍ ٱلنَّبِيِّ ٱلْفَرْدِ وَعَلَىٰ آلِهِ وَصَحْبِهِ وَسَلِّمْ تَسْلِيمًا
وَأَفْرِدْنِي بِهِ لِمَا خَلَقْتَنِي لَهُ وَاجْعَلْ لِي بِذَٰلِكَ عِزًّا
وَمَجْدًا فَرِيدًا

Allāhumma yā Allāh yā Fard ṣalli ʿalā ʿabdika wa ḥabībika sayyidinā Muḥammad al-nabiyy al-fard wa ʿalā ālihi wa ṣaḥbihi wa sallim taslīman wa afridnī bihi limā khalaqtanī la-hu wajʿal lī bi-dhālika ʿizzan wa majdan farīdā

O Allah, O Single, send prayers and abundant Peace upon Your slave and beloved, our master, Muhammad, the unrivaled Prophet, and upon his family and companions, and through him, single me out with that purpose for which You created me and make me, as a result of that, unique in honor and nobility

اَللّٰهُمَّ يَا اَللّٰهُ يَا مُقَدِّمُ صَلِّ عَلَىٰ عَبْدِكَ وَحَبِيبِكَ سَيِّدِنَا مُحَمَّدٍ ٱلنَّبِيِّ ٱلْمُقَدَّمِ وَعَلَىٰ آلِهِ وَصَحْبِهِ وَسَلِّمْ تَسْلِيمًا وَقَدِّمْنِي بِهِ فِي مَرَاتِبِ ٱلْعُبُودِيَّةِ وَٱلطَّاعَةِ لَكَ تَقْدِيمًا

Allāhumma yā Allāh yā Muqaddim ṣalli ʿalā ʿabdika wa ḥabībika sayyidinā Muḥammad al-nabiyy al-muqaddam wa ʿalā ālihi wa ṣaḥbihi wa sallim taslīman wa qaddimnī bihi fī marātib al-ʾubūdiyyah wa al-ṭāʿah laka taqdīmā

O Allah, O Expediter, send prayers and abundant Peace upon Your slave and beloved, our master, Muhammad, the advanced Prophet, and upon his family and companions, and through him, make me greatly advanced in levels of worship and obedience towards You

ٱللَّهُمَّ يَا ٱللهُ يَا مُؤَخِّرُ صَلِّ عَلَىٰ عَبْدِكَ وَحَبِيبِكَ
سَيِّدِنَا مُحَمَّدٍ ٱلنَّبِيِّ آخِرِ ٱلنَّبِيِّينَ فِي ٱلْبَعْثِ وَعَلَىٰ آلِهِ
وَصَحْبِهِ وَسَلِّمْ تَسْلِيمًا وَأَخِّرْ بِهِ عَنِّي كُلَّ سُوءٍ
فِي ٱلدَّارَيْنِ تَأْخِيرًا

Allāhumma yā Allāh yā Mu'akhkhir ṣalli 'alā 'abdika wa ḥabībika sayyidinā Muḥammad al-nabiyy ākhir al-nabiyyīn fī al-ba'th wa 'alā ālihi wa ṣaḥbihi wa sallim taslīman wa akhkhir bihi 'annī kulla sū'in fī al-dārayn ta'khīrā

O Allah, O Delayer, send prayers and abundant Peace upon Your slave and beloved, our master, Muhammad, the last Prophet to be sent, and upon his family and companions, and through him, totally suspend every ill in the two abodes

ٱللّٰهُمَّ يَا ٱللّٰهُ يَا أَوَّلُ صَلِّ عَلَىٰ عَبْدِكَ وَحَبِيبِكَ سَيِّدِنَا
مُحَمَّدٍ ٱلنَّبِيِّ ٱلْأَوَّلِ فِي ٱلْخَلْقِ وَٱلشَّفَاعَةِ وَمَرَاتِبِ
ٱلسِّيَادَةِ عَلَىٰ ٱلْخَلْقِ أَجْمَعِينَ وَعَلَىٰ آلِهِ وَصَحْبِهِ وَسَلِّمْ
تَسْلِيمًا وَاجْعَلْنِي بِهِ فِي أَوَائِلِ أَهْلِ ٱلْكَرَمِ عَلَيْكَ
وَٱلْفَضْلِ مِنْكَ وَأَوَائِلِ أَهْلِ اتِّبَاعِهِ فَضْلًا وَإِحْسَانًا

Allāhumma yā Allāh yā Awwal ṣalli ʿalā ʿabdika wa ḥabībika sayyidinā Muḥammad al-nabiyy al-awwal fī al-khalq wa al-shafāʿah wa marātib al-siyādah ʿalā al-khalq ajmaʿīn wa ʿalā ālihi wa ṣaḥbihi wa sallim taslīman wajʿalnī bihi fī awāʾil ahl al-karam ʿalayk wa al-faḍl minka wa awāʾil ahl ittibāʿihi faḍlan wa iḥsānā

O Allah, O First One, send prayers and abundant Peace upon Your slave and beloved, our master, Muhammad, the Prophet who is first in creation, intercession and levels of mastery upon all creation, and upon his family and companions, and through him, make me from the foremost people of honor to You and favor from You, and the foremost of followers of him with favor and beneficence

ٱللّٰهُمَّ يَا ٱللهُ يَا آخِرُ صَلِّ عَلَىٰ عَبْدِكَ وَحَبِيبِكَ سَيِّدِنَا
مُحَمَّدٍ ٱلنَّبِيِّ ٱلْمَبْعُوثِ إِلَىٰ آخِرِ ٱلْأُمَمِ وَخَيْرِهَا وَعَلَىٰ
آلِهِ وَصَحْبِهِ وَسَلِّمْ تَسْلِيمًا وَاجْعَلْنَا بِهِ مِنْ خَوَاصِّ
أَنْصَارِهِ وَوُرَّاثِهِ فِي آخِرِ ٱلزَّمَنِ وَمِنْ أَقْرَبِ ٱلنَّاسِ
إِلَيْهِ وَأَسْعَدِهِمْ بِهِ فِي ٱلْيَوْمِ ٱلْآخِرِ جُودًا وَكَرَمًا

Allāhumma yā Allāh yā Ākhir ṣalli ʿalā ʿabdika wa ḥabībika sayyidinā Muḥammad al-nabiyy al-mabʿūth ilā ākhir al-umam wa khayrihā wa ʿalā ālihi wa ṣaḥbihi wa sallim taslīman wajʿalnā bihi min khawāṣṣi anṣārihi wa wurrāthihi fī ākhir al-zaman wa min aqrab al-nās ilayhi wa asʿadihim bihi fī al-yawm al-ākhir jūdan wa karamā

O Allah, O Last One, send prayers and abundant Peace upon Your slave and beloved, our master, Muhammad, the Prophet who was sent to the last and best of nations, and upon his family and companions, and through him, make us from his special helpers and heirs in the end of time, and from among the most pleasing and closest of people to him, on the Day of Judgment, through generosity and honor

ٱللّٰهُمَّ يَا ٱللّٰهُ يَا ظَاهِرُ صَلِّ عَلَىٰ عَبْدِكَ وَحَبِيبِكَ
سَيِّدِنَا مُحَمَّدٍ ٱلنَّبِيِّ ٱلظَّاهِرِ وَعَلَىٰ آلِهِ وَصَحْبِهِ وَسَلِّمْ
تَسْلِيمًا وَأَرِنَا فِي حَيَاتِنَا ظُهُورَ دِينِهِ عَلَىٰ ٱلدِّينِ كُلِّهِ
وَأَظْهِرْ لَنَا بِهِ خَفِيَّاتِ ٱلْمَعَانِي فِي ٱلْفَهْمِ عَنْكَ
وَاجْعَلْ أَسْرَارَ عِنَايَتِكَ وَعِنَايَتِهِ بِنَا عَلَيْنَا ظَاهِرَةً

Allāhumma yā Allāh yā Ẓāhir ṣalli ʿalā ʿabdika wa ḥabībika sayyidinā Muḥammad al-nabiyy al-ẓāhir wa ʿalā ālihi wa ṣaḥbihi wa sallim taslīman wa arinā fī hayātinā ẓuhūra dīnihi ʿalā al-dīn kullihi wa āẓhir lanā bihi khafiyyāt al-maʿāni fī al-faḥmi ʿanka wajʿal asrāra ʿināyatika wa ʿināyatihi binā ʿalaynā ẓāhirah

O Allah, O Manifest One, send prayers and abundant Peace upon Your slave and beloved, our master, Muhammad, the manifest Prophet, and upon his family and companions, and show us, in our lifetime, the manifestation of his religion above all other religions and through him, make manifest to us the subtleties of meanings of understanding You, and through him, make the secrets of Yours and his providence for us, manifest

ٱللّٰهُمَّ يَا ٱللّٰهُ يَا بَاطِنُ صَلِّ عَلَىٰ عَبْدِكَ وَحَبِيبِكَ سَيِّدِنَا
مُحَمَّدٍ ٱلنَّبِيِّ ٱلْبَاطِنِ وَعَلَىٰ آلِهِ وَصَحْبِهِ وَسَلِّمْ تَسْلِيمًا
وَأَصْلِحْ لَنَا بِهِ كُلَّ ظَاهِرٍ وَبَاطِنٍ وَصَفِّ لَنَا ٱلْبَوَاطِنَ
وَارْزُقْنَا بِهِ حُسْنَ ٱلْاِمْتِثَالِ لِأَمْرِكَ ظَاهِرًا وَبَاطِنًا

Allāhumma yā Allāh yā Bāṭin ṣalli ʿalā ʿabdika wa ḥabībika sayyidinā Muḥammad al-nabiyy al-bāṭin wa ʿalā ālihi wa ṣaḥbihi wa sallim taslīman wa aṣliḥ lanā bihi kulla ẓāhir wa bāṭin wa ṣaffi lanā al-bawāṭin wa-urzuqnā bihi ḥusna al-imtithāli li'amrika ẓāhirā wa bāṭinā

O Allah, O Knower of the hidden, send prayers and abundant Peace upon Your slave and beloved, our master, Muhammad, the Prophet who knows the hidden, and upon his family and companions, and through him, rectify every apparent and hidden affair, and purify our inward states, and endow upon us to follow Your command accordingly, inwardly and outwardly

ٱللّٰهُمَّ يَا ٱللّٰهُ يَا وَالِي صَلِّ عَلَىٰ عَبْدِكَ وَحَبِيبِكَ
سَيِّدِنَا مُحَمَّدٍ ٱلنَّبِيِّ ٱلَّذِي جَعَلْتَهُ أَوْلَىٰ بِٱلْمُؤْمِنِينَ
مِنْ أَنْفُسِهِمْ وَعَلَىٰ آلِهِ وَصَحْبِهِ وَسَلِّمْ تَسْلِيمًا وَتَوَلَّنَا
بِهِ فِي جَمِيعِ أُمُورِنَا وَوَلِّ عَلَىٰ ٱلْمُسْلِمِينَ خِيَارَهُمْ
وَاصْرِفْ عَنْهُمْ شِرَارَهُمْ سِرًّا وَعَلَنًا

Allāhumma yā Allāh yā Wālī ṣalli ʿalā ʿabdika wa ḥabībika sayyidinā Muḥammad al-nabiyy al-ladhī jaʿaltahu awlā bil-muʾminīn min anfusihim wa ʿalā ālihi wa ṣaḥbihi wa sallim taslīman wa tawallanā bihi fī jamīʿ umūrinā wa walli ʿalā al-muslimīn khiyārahum wa-iṣrif ʿanhum shirārahum sirran wa ʿalanā

O Allah, O Patron, send prayers and abundant Peace upon Your slave and beloved, our master, Muhammad, the Prophet who You made closer to the believers than their own selves, and upon his family and companions, and through him, take control of all our affairs and appoint a ruler, for the Muslims, from among the best, and avert from them those who are evil, in public and private

ٱللّٰهُمَّ يَا ٱللهُ يَا مُتَعَالُ صَلِّ عَلَىٰ عَبْدِكَ وَحَبِيبِكَ سَيِّدِنَا مُحَمَّدٍ ٱلنَّبِيِّ ٱلَّذِي تَعَالَتْ رُتْبَتُهُ وَمَكَانَتُهُ وَعَلَىٰ آلِهِ وَصَحْبِهِ وَسَلِّمْ تَسْلِيمًا وَارْفَعْنَا فِي مَرَاتِبِ قُرْبِكَ ٱلْعَالِيَةِ رِفْعًا

Allāhumma yā Allāh yā Muta'āl ṣalli 'alā 'abdika wa ḥabībika sayyidinā Muḥammad al-nabiyy al-ladhī ta'ālat rutbatuhu wa makānatuhu wa 'alā ālihi wa ṣaḥbihi wa sallim taslīman wa-irfa'nā fī qurbik al-'āliyah rif'ā

O Allah, O Self Exalted, send prayers and abundant Peace upon Your slave and beloved, our master, Muhammad, the Prophet whose degree and rank You elevated, and upon his family and companions, and through him, elevate us to Your elevated ranks of proximity

ٱللّٰهُمَّ يَا ٱللّٰهُ يَا بَرُّ صَلِّ عَلَىٰ عَبْدِكَ وَحَبِيبِكَ سَيِّدِنَا مُحَمَّدٍ ٱلنَّبِيِّ ٱلْبَرِّ وَعَلَىٰ آلِهِ وَصَحْبِهِ وَسَلِّمْ تَسْلِيمًا وَكُنْ لَنَا بِهِ بَرًّا رَؤُوفًا

Allāhumma yā Allāh yā Barr ṣalli ʿalā ʿabdika wa ḥabībika sayyidinā Muḥammad al-nabiyy al-barr wa ʿalā ālihi wa ṣaḥbihi wa sallim taslīman wa kun lanā bihi barran raʾūfā

O Allah, O source of Goodness, send prayers and abundant Peace upon Your slave and beloved, our master, Muhammad, the Prophet who is the source of goodness, and upon his family and companions, and through him, be a source of goodness for us, compassionately

NUMBER FIFTY-NINE

ٱللَّهُمَّ يَا ٱللّٰهُ يَا تَوَّابُ صَلِّ عَلَىٰ عَبْدِكَ وَحَبِيبِكَ
سَيِّدِنَا مُحَمَّدٍ ٱلنَّبِيِّ ٱلتَّوَّابِ وَعَلَىٰ آلِهِ وَصَحْبِهِ وَسَلِّمْ
تَسْلِيمًا وَاجْعَلْنِي بِهَا إِلَيْكَ تَوَّابًا فِي كُلِّ نَفَسٍ مُخْلِصًا
صَادِقًا مَحْبُوبًا

Allāhumma yā Allāh yā Tawwāb ṣalli ʿalā ʿabdika wa ḥabībika sayyidinā Muḥammad al-nabiyy al-tawwab wa ʿalā ālihi wa ṣaḥbihi wa sallim taslīman, wajʿalnī bihā ilayka tawwāban fī kulli nafasin mukhliṣan ṣādiqan maḥbūbā

O Allah, O Ever-pardoning, send prayers and abundant Peace upon Your slave and beloved, our master, Muhammad, the ever-pardoning Prophet, and upon his family and companions, and through him, make us sincerely, truthfully and with love, repentant towards You in every breath

ٱللّٰهُمَّ يَا ٱللّٰهُ يَا عَفُوُّ صَلِّ عَلَىٰ عَبْدِكَ وَحَبِيبِكَ سَيِّدِنَا مُحَمَّدٍ ٱلنَّبِيِّ ٱلْعَفُوِّ وَعَلَىٰ آلِهِ وَصَحْبِهِ وَسَلِّمْ تَسْلِيمًا وَاعْفُ بِهِ عَنَّا وَاجْعَلْنَا مِمَّنْ عَفَا وَأَصْلَحَ فَجَعَلْتَ أَجْرَهُ عَلَيْكَ وَسَعْيَهُ عِنْدَكَ مَشْكُورًا

Allāhumma yā Allāh yā ʿAfū ṣalli ʿalā ʿabdika wa ḥabībika sayyidinā Muḥammad al-nabiyy al-ʿafū wa ʿalā ālihi wa ṣaḥbihi wa sallim taslīman waʾfu bihi ʿannā wajʾalnā mimman ʿafā wa aṣlaha fajaʾalta ajrahu ʿalayk wa saʾyahū ʿindaka mashkūrā

O Allah, O Pardoner, send prayers and abundant Peace upon Your slave and beloved, our master, Muhammad, the pardoning Prophet, and upon his family and companions and through him, pardon us and make us among those who pardoned, reconciled with others and whose reward and efforts were accepted

ٱللّٰهُمَّ يَا ٱللّٰهُ يَا رَؤُوفُ صَلِّ عَلَىٰ عَبْدِكَ وَحَبِيبِكَ
سَيِّدِنَا مُحَمَّدٍ ٱلنَّبِيِّ ٱلرَّؤُوفِ وَعَلَىٰ آلِهِ وَصَحْبِهِ وَسَلِّمْ
تَسْلِيمًا وَوَفِّرْ حَظَّنَا مِنْ رَأْفَتِكَ وَكُنْ بِنَا وَبِٱلْمُؤْمِنِينَ
رَؤُوفًا رَحِيمًا

Allāhumma yā Allāh yā Ra'ūf ṣalli 'alā 'abdika wa ḥabībika sayyidinā Muḥammad al-nabiyy al-raūf wa 'alā ālihi wa ṣaḥbihi wa sallim taslīman wa waffir ḥaẓẓanā min ra'fatik wa kun binā wa bi-al-mu'minīn ra'ūfān raḥīmā

O Allah, O Compassionate, send prayers and abundant Peace upon Your slave and beloved, our master, Muhammad, the compassionate Prophet, and upon his family and companions, and through him, apportion for us from Your compassion and be immensely compassionate and merciful towards us, and the believers

ٱللّٰهُمَّ يَا ٱللّٰهُ يَا ذَا ٱلْجَلَالِ وَٱلْإِكْرَامِ صَلِّ عَلَىٰ عَبْدِكَ
وَحَبِيبِكَ سَيِّدِنَا مُحَمَّدٍ ٱلنَّبِيِّ ٱلْجَلِيلِ ٱلْكَرِيمِ وَعَلَىٰ
آلِهِ وَصَحْبِهِ وَسَلِّمْ تَسْلِيمًا وَهَبْ لَنَا بِهِ جَلَالًا وَجَمَالًا
وَكَمَالًا وَإِكْرَامًا وَأَكْرِمْنَا بِمَا أَنْتَ أَهْلُهُ أَبَدًا سَرْمَدًا

Allāhumma yā Allāh yā Dhal-Jalāli wal-Ikrām ṣalli ʿalā ʿabdika wa ḥabībika sayyidinā Muḥammad al-nabiyy al-jalīl al-karīm wa ʿalā ālihi wa ṣaḥbihi wa sallim taslīman wa hab lanā bihi jalālan wa jamālan wa kamālan wa ikrāman wa akrimnā bi-mā anta ahluhu abadan sarmadā

O Allah, O Lord of Majesty and Honor, send prayers and abundant Peace upon Your slave and beloved, our master, Muhammad, the majestic and honorable Prophet, and upon his family and companions, and through him, bestow upon us majesty, perfection and honor us in the way which is befitting of You, forever and ever

ٱللّٰهُمَّ يَا ٱللّٰهُ يَا مُقْسِطُ صَلِّ عَلَىٰ عَبْدِكَ وَحَبِيبِكَ سَيِّدِنَا مُحَمَّدٍ ٱلنَّبِيِّ ٱلْمُقْسِطِ وَعَلَىٰ آلِهِ وَصَحْبِهِ وَسَلِّمْ تَسْلِيمًا وَاجْعَلْنِي بِهِ مُقْسِطًا وَمُنْصِفًا حَكِيمًا

Allāhumma yā Allāh yā Muqsiṭ ṣalli ʿalā ʿabdika wa ḥabībika sayyidinā Muḥammad al-nabiyy al-muqsiṭ wa ʿalā ālihi wa ṣaḥbihi wa sallim taslīman wajʿalnī bihi muqsiṭan wa munṣifan hakīmā

O Allah, O Requiter, send prayers and abundant Peace upon Your slave and beloved, our master, Muhammad, the requitable Prophet, and upon his family and companions, and through him, make me one who is requitable, righteous and wise

ٱللَّهُمَّ يَا ٱللهُ يَا جَامِعُ صَلِّ عَلَىٰ عَبْدِكَ وَحَبِيبِكَ
سَيِّدِنَا مُحَمَّدٍ ٱلنَّبِيِّ ٱلْجَامِعِ لِأَسْرَارِكَ وَعَلَىٰ آلِهِ وَصَحْبِهِ
وَسَلِّمْ تَسْلِيمًا وَٱجْمَعْ لِي بِهِ بَيْنَ خَيْرَاتِ وَسَعَادَاتِ
ٱلدَّارَيْنِ وَٱجْمَعْ بِهِ شَمْلِي وَٱجْمَعْنِي بِهِ عَلَيْكَ جَمْعًا

Allāhumma yā Allāh yā Jāmi' ṣalli 'alā 'abdika wa ḥabībika sayyidinā Muḥammad al-nabiyy al-jāmi' li-asrārik wa 'alā ālihi wa ṣaḥbihi wa sallim wajma' lī bihi bayna khayrāt wa sa'ādāt al-dārayn wajma' bihi shamlī wajma'nī bihi alayka jam'ā.

O Allah, O Gatherer, send prayers and abundant Peace upon Your slave and beloved, our master, Muhammad, the Prophet who gathered all of Your secrets, and upon his family and companions, and through him, gather for us the good and bliss of the two abodes, and through him, unite my matters and through him, entirely unite me upon You

NUMBER SIXTY-FIVE

ٱللَّهُمَّ يَا ٱللَّٰهُ يَا غَنِيُّ صَلِّ عَلَىٰ عَبْدِكَ وَحَبِيبِكَ سَيِّدِنَا
مُحَمَّدٍ ٱلنَّبِيِّ ٱلْغَنِيِّ بِكَ وَأَعْظَمِ خَلْقِكَ إِفْتِقَارًا إِلَيْكَ
وَعَلَىٰ آلِهِ وَصَحْبِهِ وَسَلِّمْ تَسْلِيمًا وَأَغْنِنِي بِحَلَالِكَ عَنْ
حَرَامِكَ وَبِطَاعَتِكَ عَنْ مَعْصِيَتِكَ وَارْزُقْنِي غِنَى ٱلْقَلْبِ

Allāhumma yā Allāh yā Ghaniyy ṣalli ʿalā ʿabdika wa ḥabībika sayyidinā Muḥammad al-nabiyy al-ghanī bika wa aʿẓami khalqika iftiqāran ilayka wa ʿalā ālihi wa ṣaḥbihi wa sallim taslīman wa aghninī bi-ḥalālika ʿan ḥarāmika wa bi ṭāʿatika ʿan maʿṣiyatika wa-urzuqnī ghinā al-qalb

O Allah, O Self-sufficient, send prayers and abundant Peace upon Your slave and beloved, our master, Muhammad, the Prophet who is self-sufficient through You, the greatest of Your creation of those who are dependent upon You, and upon his family and companions, and through him, suffice us with that which is legally permissible with You, over that which is legally impermissible with You and obedience towards You over disobedience towards you

اَللّٰهُمَّ يَا اَللّٰهُ يَا مُغْنِي صَلِّ عَلَىٰ عَبْدِكَ وَحَبِيبِكَ
سَيِّدِنَا مُحَمَّدٍ اَلنَّبِيِّ اَلْمُغْنِي بِإِذْنِكَ مِنْ فَضْلِكَ عَلَىٰ
مَنْ شِئْتَ مِنْ عِبَادِكَ وَعَلَىٰ آلِهِ وَصَحْبِهِ وَسَلِّمْ تَسْلِيمًا
وَأَغْنِنِي بِهِ وَبِبَرَكَاتِهِ وَوَجَاهَتِهِ بِفَضْلِكَ عَمَّنْ سِوَاكَ

Allāhumma yā Allāh yā Mughniyy ṣalli ʿalā ʿabdika wa ḥabībika sayyidinā Muḥammad al-nabiyy al-mughnī bi-idhnika min faḍlika ʿalā man shi'ta min ʿibādika wa ʿalā ālihi wa ṣaḥbihi wa sallim taslīman wa aghninī bihi wa bi-barakātihi wa wajāhatihī bi- faḍlika ʿamman siwāk

O Allah, O Enricher, send prayers and abundant Peace upon Your slave and beloved, our master, Muhammad, the enriching Prophet, by your permission, towards whomsoever of Your servants You will, with Your Bounty, and upon his family and companions, and make me self-sufficient from others, through him, his blessings and stature, through Your Bounty

ٱللّٰهُمَّ يَا ٱللّٰهُ يَا مَانِعُ صَلِّ عَلَىٰ عَبْدِكَ وَحَبِيبِكَ سَيِّدِنَا مُحَمَّدٍ ٱلنَّبِيِّ حِصْنِكَ ٱلْمَانِعِ ٱلْحَصِينِ وَعَلَىٰ آلِهِ وَصَحْبِهِ وَسَلِّمْ تَسْلِيمًا وَامْنَعْ بِهِ عَنِّي جَمِيعَ ٱلْأَسْوَاءِ مَنْعًا

Allāhumma yā Allāh yā Māni' ṣalli 'alā 'abdika wa ḥabībika sayyidinā Muḥammad al-nabiyy ḥiṣnik al-māni' al-ḥaṣīn wa 'alā ālihi wa ṣaḥbihi wa sallim taslīman wa-imna' bihi 'annī jamī' al-aswā'i man'ā

O Allah, O Shielder, send prayers and abundant Peace upon Your slave and beloved, our master, Muhammad, the Prophet who is Your fortified preventative shield, and upon his family and companions, and through him, totally shield me from all evil

ٱللَّهُمَّ يَا ٱللهُ يَا نَافِعُ صَلِّ عَلَىٰ عَبْدِكَ وَحَبِيبِكَ سَيِّدِنَا
مُحَمَّدٍ ٱلنَّبِيِّ ٱلنَّافِعِ مَنْبَعِ ٱلْمَنَافِعِ وَعَلَىٰ آلِهِ وَصَحْبِهِ
وَسَلِّمْ تَسْلِيمًا وَاجْمَعْ لِي بِهِ ٱلْمَنَافِعَ وَاجْعَلْنِي بِهِ مِنْ
أَنْفَعِ خَلْقِكَ لِخَلْقِكَ ظَاهِرًا وَبَاطِنًا

Allāhumma yā Nāfiʿ ṣalli ʿalā ʿabdika wa ḥabībika sayyidinā Muḥammad al-nabiyy al-nāfiʿ manbaʿ il-manāfiʿ wa ʿalā ālihi wa ṣaḥbihi wa sallim taslīman wajmaʿ lī bihi al-manāfiʿ wajʿalnī bihi min anfaʿi khalqika li-khalqika ẓāhiran wa bāṭinā

O Allah, O Advantageous one, send prayers and abundant Peace upon Your slave and beloved, our master, Muhammad, the advantageous Prophet who is the source of benefits, and upon his family and companions, and through him, gather for me benefits, and through him, make me among the most beneficial of Your creation towards Your creation, outwardly and inwardly

ٱللَّٰهُمَّ يَا ٱللَّٰهُ يَا نُورُ صَلِّ عَلَىٰ عَبْدِكَ وَحَبِيبِكَ سَيِّدِنَا
مُحَمَّدٍ ٱلنَّبِيِّ نُورِكَ ٱلْأَزْهَرِ ٱلسَّارِي وَمَدَدِكَ ٱلْأَكْبَرِ
ٱلْجَارِي وَعَلَىٰ آلِهِ وَصَحْبِهِ وَسَلِّمْ تَسْلِيمًا وَاجْعَلْ بِهِ
فِي قَلْبِي نُورًا، وَفِي قَبْرِي نُورًا، وَفِي سَمْعِي نُورًا، وَفِي
بَصَرِي نُورًا، وَفِي شَعْرِي نُورًا، وَفِي بَشَرِي نُورًا، وَفِي
لَحْمِي نُورًا، وَفِي دَمِي نُورًا، وَفِي عِظَامِي نُورًا، وَفِي
عَصَبِي نُورًا، وَمِنْ بَيْنِ يَدَيَّ نُورًا، وَمِنْ خَلْفِي نُورًا،
وَعَنْ يَمِينِي نُورًا، وَعَنْ شِمَالِي نُورًا، وَمِنْ فَوْقِي نُورًا،
وَمِنْ تَحْتِي نُورًا، ٱللَّٰهُمَّ زِدْنِي نُورًا، وَأَعْطِنِي نُورًا،
وَاجْعَلْنِي بِهِ نُورًا، وَنَوِّرْ بِهِ جَمِيعَ أَحْوَالِي وَشُؤُونِي
فِي ٱلدَّارَيْنِ تَنْوِيرًا

Allāhumma yā Allāh yā Nūr ṣalli ʿalā ʿabdika wa ḥabībika sayyidinā Muḥammad al-nabiyy nūrik al-azhar al-sārī wa madadik al-akbar al-jārī wa ʿalā ālihi wa ṣaḥbihi wa sallim taslīman wajʿal bihi fī qalbī nūrā, wa fī qabrī nūrā, wa fī samʿī nūrā, wa fī baṣarī nūrā, wa fī shaʿrī nūrā, wa fī basharī nūrā, wa fī laḥmī nūrā, wa fī damī nūrā, wa fī iẓāmī nūrā, wa fī ʿaṣabī nūrā, wa min bayni yadayy nūrā, wa min khalfī nūrā, wa ʿan yamīnī nūrā wa ʿan shimālī nūrā, wa min fawqī nūrā, wa min taḥtī nūrā, Allāhumma zidnī nūrā, wa aʿaṭinī nūrā, wajʿalnī bihi nūrā, wa nawwir bihi jamīʾ aḥwālī wa shuʾūnī fī al-dārayn tanwīrā

O Allah, O Illuminator, send prayers and abundant Peace upon Your slave and beloved, our master, Muhammad, the Prophet who is Your luminous light which spreads and from whom flows the greatest assistance, and upon his family and companions, and through him, illuminate my heart, my grave, my ears, my eyes, my hair, my skin, my flesh, my blood, my bones and my veins, and illuminate in front of me, behind me, on my right side, on my left side, above me and underneath me. O Allah increase me in light, grant me light and through him, make me illuminated and immensely illuminate all my states and affairs in the two abodes

ٱللَّهُمَّ يَا ٱللهُ يَا هَادِي صَلِّ عَلَىٰ عَبْدِكَ وَحَبِيبِكَ
سَيِّدِنَا مُحَمَّدٍ ٱلنَّبِيِّ ٱلْهَادِي وَعَلَىٰ آلِهِ وَصَحْبِهِ وَسَلِّمْ
تَسْلِيمًا، وَاهْدِنِي بِهِ سُبُلَ ٱلسَّلَامِ، وَاهْدِنِي بِهِ إِلَىٰ
صِرَاطِكَ ٱلْمُسْتَقِيمِ، وَاهْدِنِي وَاهْدِ بِي لِنُورِكَ،
وَاهْدِنِي بِهِ إِلَيْكَ وَاجْعَلْنِي بِهِ هَادِيًا مَهْدِيًّا

Allāhumma yā Allāh yā Hādī ṣalli ʿalā ʿabdika wa ḥabībika sayyidinā Muḥammad al-nabiyy al-hādī wa ʿalā ālihi wa ṣaḥbihi wa sallim taslīman, wahdinī bihi subul al-salām, wahdinī bihi ilā ṣirāṭik al-mustaqīm, wahdinī wahdi bī li-nūrik, wahdinī bihi ilayk wajʿalnī bihi hādiyan mahdiyyā

O Allah, O Guiding One, send prayers and abundant Peace upon Your slave and beloved, our master, Muhammad, the guiding Prophet, and upon his family and companions, and through him, guide me to the path of peace, and through him, guide me to Your straight path and guide me and cause me to guide to Your light, and through him, guide me towards You and through him, make me a guiding guide

ٱللّٰهُمَّ يَا ٱللّٰهُ يَا بَدِيعُ صَلِّ عَلَىٰ عَبْدِكَ وَحَبِيبِكَ
سَيِّدِنَا مُحَمَّدٍ ٱلنَّبِيِّ أَبْدَعِ خَلْقِكَ رُوحًا وَجِسْمًا
حِسًّا وَمَعْنًى ظَاهِرًا وَبَاطِنًا أَوَّلًا وَآخِرًا وَعَلَىٰ آلِهِ
وَصَحْبِهِ وَسَلِّمْ تَسْلِيمًا، وَهَبْ لِي بِهِ بَدَائِعَ ٱلْمَعَارِفِ
وَٱلْعُلُومِ وَالشُّهُودِ ٱلْأَسْنَىٰ وَمَكِّنِي بِهِ تَمْكِينًا

Allāhumma yā Allāh yā Badī' ṣalli ʿalā ʿabdika wa ḥabībika sayyidinā Muḥammad al-nabiyy abdaʿ khalqika rūhan wa jisman ḥissan wa maʿnan ẓāhiran wa bāṭinā awwalan wa ākhiran wa ʿalā ālihi wa ṣaḥbihi wa sallim taslīman, wa hab lī bihi badāʾiʿa al-maʿārif wal-ʿulūm wal-shuhūd il-asnā wa makkinī bihi tamkīnā

O Allah, O Incomparable Originator, send prayers and abundant Peace upon Your slave and beloved, our master, Muhammad, the Prophet who is the most incomparable of Your creation in terms of soul and body, outwardly and inwardly, externally and internally, first and last, and upon his family and companions, and through him, endow upon me amazing gnosis, sciences, splendored witnessing, and through him make me firmly established

ٱللّٰهُمَّ يَا ٱللهُ يَا وَارِثُ صَلِّ عَلَىٰ عَبْدِكَ وَحَبِيبِكَ
سَيِّدِنَا مُحَمَّدٍ ٱلنَّبِيِّ أَعْظَمِ وَارِثٍ لِكِتَابِكَ ٱلْمُهَيْمِنِ
ٱلْكَرِيمِ ٱلْمَجِيدِ ٱلْعَظِيمِ وَمُوَرِّثٍ لِأَسْرَارِهِ وَعَلَىٰ آلِهِ
وَصَحْبِهِ وَسَلِّمْ تَسْلِيمًا، وَاجْعَلْ سَهْمِي مِنْ إِرْثِهِ سَهْمًا
جَسِيمًا فَخِيمًا وَحَظِّي مِنْهُ حَظًّا وَافِرًا عَظِيمًا

Allāhumma yā Allāh yā Wārith ṣalli ʿalā ʿabdika wa ḥabībika sayyidinā Muḥammad al-nabiyy aʿadham wārithin li-kitābik al-muhaymin al-karīm al-majīd al-ʾaẓīm wa muwarrithin li-asrārihi wa ʿalā ālihi wa ṣaḥbihi wa sallim taslīman, wajʿal sahmī min irthihi sahman jasīman fakhīmā wa ḥaẓẓī minhu ḥaẓẓan wāfiran ʿadhīmā

O Allah, O Inheritor, send prayers and abundant Peace upon Your slave and beloved, our master, Muhammad, the Prophet who is the greatest inheritor of Your reliable, noble, mighty and great book, and the legator of its secrets, and upon his family and companions, and through him, make my portion of inheritance from him, huge and splendid, and my share from him, great and plentiful

ٱللَّهُمَّ يَا ٱللهُ يَا رَشِيدُ صَلِّ عَلَىٰ عَبْدِكَ وَحَبِيبِكَ
سَيِّدِنَا مُحَمَّدٍ ٱلنَّبِيِّ ٱلرَّشِيدِ وَعَلَىٰ آلِهِ وَصَحْبِهِ وَسَلِّمْ
تَسْلِيمًا، وَأَلْهِمْنِي بِهِ رُشْدِي وَارْزُقْنِي نَشْرَ ٱلرُّشْدِ فِي
ٱلْخَلْقِ خُصُوصًا وَعُمُومًا وَهَيِّئْ لِي بِهِ مِنْ أَمْرِي رَشَدًا

Allāhumma yā Allāh yā Rashīd ṣalli ʿalā ʿabdika wa ḥabībika sayyidinā Muḥammad al-nabiyy al-rashīd wa ʿalā ālihi wa ṣaḥbihi wa sallim taslīman, wa alhimnī bihi rushdī warzuqnī nashr al-rushd fil-khalq khuṣūṣan wa ʿumūman wa hayyiʾ lī bihi min amrī rashadā

O Allah, O Guide, send prayers and abundant Peace upon Your slave and beloved, our master, Muhammad, the guiding Prophet, and upon his family and companions, and through him, inspire me to be rightly guided, and endow upon me to spread true steadfastness to the creation, the common and the special among them, and through him, prepare for me to have a guided affair

ٱللّٰهُمَّ يَا ٱللهُ يَا صَبُورُ صَلِّ عَلَىٰ عَبْدِكَ وَحَبِيبِكَ
سَيِّدِنَا مُحَمَّدٍ ٱلنَّبِيِّ ٱلصَّبُورِ وَعَلَىٰ آلِهِ وَصَحْبِهِ وَسَلِّمْ
تَسْلِيمًا وَاجْعَلْنِي بِهِ مِنْ ٱلصَّابِرِينَ ٱلَّذِينَ يُؤْتَوْنَ
أَجْرَهُمْ بِغَيْرِ حِسَابٍ فِي خَيْرٍ وَلُطْفٍ وَعَافِيَةٍ
إِحْسَانًا وَكَرَمًا

Allāhumma yā Allāh yā Ṣabūr ṣalli ʿalā ʿabdika wa ḥabībika sayyidinā Muḥammad al-nabiyy al-ṣabūr wa ʿalā ālihi wa ṣaḥbihi wa sallim taslīman, wajʿalnī bihi min aṣ-ṣābirīn al-ladhīna yuʾtawna ajrahum bi-ghayri ḥisāb fī khayr wa luṭf wa ʿāfiyah iḥsānan wa karamā

O Allah, O Patient One, send prayers and abundant Peace upon Your slave and beloved, our master, Muhammad, the patient Prophet, and upon his family and companions, and through him, make me from the patient who receive their reward without reckoning, with goodness, gentleness, forgiveness and well-being, with beneficence and generosity

ٱللَّهُمَّ يَا ٱللهُ يَا طَاهِرُ صَلِّ عَلَىٰ عَبْدِكَ وَحَبِيبِكَ
سَيِّدِنَا مُحَمَّدٍ ٱلنَّبِيِّ ٱلطَّاهِرِ وَعَلَىٰ آلِهِ وَصَحْبِهِ وَسَلِّمْ
تَسْلِيمًا وَطَهِّرْنِي بِهِ تَطْهِيرًا

Allāhumma yā Allāh yā Ṭāhir ṣalli ʿalā ʿabdika wa ḥabībika sayyidinā Muḥammad al-nabiyy al-ṭāhir wa ʿalā ālihi wa ṣaḥbihi wa sallim taslīman, wa ṭahhirnī bihi taṭhīrā

Allah, O Pure One, send prayers and abundant Peace upon Your slave and beloved, our master, Muhammad, the pure Prophet, and upon his family and companions, and through him, completely purify me

ٱللّٰهُمَّ يَا ٱللّٰهُ يَا طَيِّبُ صَلِّ عَلَىٰ عَبْدِكَ وَحَبِيبِكَ
سَيِّدِنَا مُحَمَّدٍ ٱلنَّبِيِّ ٱلطَّيِّبِ وَعَلَىٰ آلِهِ وَصَحْبِهِ وَسَلِّمْ
تَسْلِيمًا وطَيِّبْنِي بِهِ تَطْيِيبًا

Allāhumma yā Allāh yā Ṭayyib ṣalli ʿalā ʿabdika wa ḥabībika sayyidinā Muḥammad al-nabiyy al-ṭayyib wa ʿalā ālihi wa ṣaḥbihi wa sallim taslīman, wa ṭayyibnī bihi taṭyībā

O Allah, O One of Goodness, send prayers and abundant Peace upon Your slave and beloved, our master, Muhammad, the Prophet of goodness, and upon his family and companions, and through him, grant me goodness, extensively

ٱللّٰهُمَّ يَا ٱللهُ يَا حَنَّانُ صَلِّ عَلَىٰ عَبْدِكَ وَحَبِيبِكَ
سَيِّدِنَا مُحَمَّدٍ ٱلنَّبِيِّ وَاسِعِ ٱلْحُنَّانِ وَعَلَىٰ آلِهِ وَصَحْبِهِ
وَسَلِّمْ تَسْلِيمًا وَتَحَنَّنْ عَلَيَّ بِهِ تَحَنُّنًا

Allāhumma yā Allāh yā Ḥannān ṣalli ʿalā ʿabdika wa ḥabībika sayyidinā Muḥammad al-nabiyy wāsiʿ al-ḥannān wa ʿalā ālihi wa ṣaḥbihi wa sallim taslīman wa taḥannan ʿalayya bihi taḥannunā

O Allah, O Affectionate One, send prayers and abundant Peace upon Your slave and beloved, our master, Muhammad, the vastly affectionate Prophet, and upon his family and companions, and through him, immensely show me affection

ٱللَّهُمَّ يَا ٱللَّهُ يَا مَنَّانُ صَلِّ عَلَىٰ عَبْدِكَ وَحَبِيبِكَ
سَيِّدِنَا مُحَمَّدٍ ٱلنَّبِيِّ مِنَّتِكَ ٱلْكُبْرَىٰ عَلَىٰ خَلْقِكَ
وَعَلَىٰ آلِهِ وَصَحْبِهِ وَسَلِّمْ تَسْلِيمًا وَهَبْ لِي بِهِ وَاسِعَ
ٱلْإِمْتِنَانِ وَعَظِيمَ ٱلْمَنِّ ظَاهِرًا وَبَاطِنًا

Allāhumma yā Allāh yā Mannān ṣalli ʿalā ʿabdika wa ḥabībika sayyidinā Muḥammad al-nabiyy minnatik al-kubrá ʿalā khalqik wa ʿalā ālihi wa ṣaḥbihi wa sallim taslīman, wa hab lī bihi wāsiʿ al-imtinān wa ʿaẓīm al-mānni ẓāhiran wa bāṭinā

O Allah, O Benefactor, send prayers and abundant Peace upon Your slave and beloved, our master, Muhammad, the Prophet who is the greatest of Your gifts to creation, and upon his family and companions, and through him, grant me vast gifts and great favor outwardly and inwardly

ٱللَّهُمَّ يَا ٱللهُ يَا مُتَفَضِّلُ صَلِّ عَلَىٰ عَبْدِكَ وَحَبِيبِكَ
سَيِّدِنَا مُحَمَّدٍ ٱلنَّبِيِّ ٱلْمُتَفَضِّلِ وَعَلَىٰ آلِهِ وَصَحْبِهِ وَسَلِّمْ
تَسْلِيمًا وَآتِنِي مِن لَّدُنْكَ فَضْلًا عَظِيمًا وَخُذْ بِيَدِي
إِلَيْكَ أَخْذَ أَهْلِ ٱلْفَضْلِ عَلَيْكَ فَضْلًا وَإِحْسَانًا

Allāhumma yā Allāh yā Mutafaḍḍil ṣalli ʿalā ʿabdika wa ḥabībika sayyidinā Muḥammad al-nabiyy al-mutafaḍḍil wa ʿalā ālihi wa ṣaḥbihi wa sallim taslīman wa ātinī min ladunka faḍlan ʿaẓīma wa khudh bi yadī ilayka akhdha ahl al-faḍli ʿalayk faḍlan wa iḥsānā

O Allah, O Giver of Beneficence, send prayers and abundant Peace upon Your slave and beloved, our master, Muhammad, the Prophet of beneficence and upon his family and companions, and through him, grant me vast beneficence from You, and make me from the people of beneficence in Your presence, and elevate me to the highest ranks of beneficence through generosity and kindness

ٱللّٰهُمَّ يَا ٱللهُ يَا مُحْسِنُ صَلِّ عَلَىٰ عَبْدِكَ وَحَبِيبِكَ
سَيِّدِنَا مُحَمَّدٍ ٱلنَّبِيِّ ٱلْمُحْسِنِ وَعَلَىٰ آلِهِ وَصَحْبِهِ وَسَلِّمْ
تَسْلِيمًا وَهَبْ لِي بِهِ مِنْكَ إِحْسَانًا وَاسِعًا وَاجْعَلْنِي
عِنْدَكَ مِنَ ٱلْمُحْسِنِينَ وَارْفَعْنِي إِلَىٰ أَعْلَىٰ مَرَاتِبِ
ٱلْإِحْسَانِ جُودًا وَكَرَمًا

Allāhumma yā Allāh yā Muḥsin ṣalli ʿalā ʿabdika wa ḥabībika sayyidinā Muḥammad al-nabiyy al-muḥsin wa ʿalā ālihi wa ṣaḥbihi wa sallim taslīman, wa hab lī bihi minka iḥsānan wāsiʿā, wajʿalnī ʿindaka min al-muḥsinīn, warfaʿnī ilá aʿalā marātib il-iḥsān jūdan wa karamā

O Allah, O Beneficent One, send prayers and abundant Peace upon Your slave and beloved, our master, Muhammad, the beneficent Prophet, and upon his family and companions, and through him, grant me, from You, great beneficence and take me, in a manner of the people of beneficence, by the hand, towards You with generosity and kindness

ٱللَّهُمَّ يَا ٱللهُ يَا مُنْعِمُ صَلِّ عَلَىٰ عَبْدِكَ وَحَبِيبِكَ سَيِّدِنَا مُحَمَّدٍ ٱلنَّبِيِّ ٱلنِّعْمَةِ ٱلْعُظْمَىٰ وَعَلَىٰ آلِهِ وَصَحْبِهِ وَسَلِّمْ تَسْلِيمًا وَوَسِّعْ عَلَيَّ نِعَمَكَ وَارْزُقْنِي شُكْرَهَا وَاحْفَظْهَا مِنَ ٱلزَّوَالِ وَأَنْعِمْ عَلَيَّ بِمَا أَنْتَ أَهْلُهُ فِي كُلِّ حِينٍ وَحَالٍ ظَاهِرًا وَبَاطِنًا

Allāhumma yā Allāh yā Mun'im ṣalli 'alā 'abdika wa ḥabībika sayyidinā Muḥammad al-nabiyy al-ni'mah al-'uẓmā wa 'alā ālihi wa ṣaḥbihi wa sallim taslīman wa wassi' 'alayy ni'amak wa-urzuqnī shukrahā wahfaẓhā min al-zawāl wa an'im 'alayy bimā anta ahluhu fī kulli hīn wa hāl ẓāhiran wa bāṭinā

O Allah, O Bestower of blessings, send prayers and abundant Peace upon Your slave and beloved, our master, Muhammad, the Prophet who is the greatest blessing, and upon his family and companions, and through him, expand Your blessings upon me, endow me with gratitude for them, protect them from disappearing, and bless me with that which is befitting of You in every time and condition, outwardly and inwardly

ٱللَّهُمَّ يَا ٱللهُ يَا جَوَّادُ صَلِّ عَلَىٰ عَبْدِكَ وَحَبِيبِكَ
سَيِّدِنَا مُحَمَّدٍ ٱلنَّبِيِّ ٱلْجَوَّادِ وَعَلَىٰ آلِهِ وَصَحْبِهِ وَسَلِّمْ
تَسْلِيمًا وَضَاعِفْ عَلَيَّ جُودَكَ وَجُدْ عَلَيَّ فِي ٱلدَّارَيْنِ
بِمَا أَنْتَ أَهْلُهُ وأَثْبِتْنِي عِنْدَكَ فِي ٱلْعِبَادِ ٱلْأَجْوَادِ
جُودًا وَامْتِنَانًا

Allāhumma yā Allāh yā Jawwād ṣalli ʿalā ʿabdika wa ḥabībika sayyidinā Muḥammad al-nabiyy al-jawwād wa ʿalā ālihi wa ṣaḥbihi wa sallim taslīman, wa ḍāʿif ʿalayya jūdak, wa jud ʿalayya fil-dārayn bi-mā anta ahluhu wa athbitnī ʿindaka fī al-ʾibād al-ajwād jūdan wamtinānā

O Allah, O Generous One, send prayers and abundant Peace upon Your slave and beloved, our master, Muhammad, the generous Prophet, and upon his family and companions, and multiply Your generosity upon me, show generosity upon me in the two abodes with that which is befitting of You and firmly establish me with You, from among Your generous slaves, with generosity and grace

APPENDIX 1

Insights into Sending prayers Upon the Prophet ﷺ

Ḥabīb ʿUmar bin Hafīẓ (may Allah ﷻ protect him and benefit us through him) provides some valuable insights into sending prayers upon the Prophet ﷺ. Extracts from a lesson during the Dawah Conference, Dar al-Mustafa, Muharram 1433 / December 2011.

The Reality of Sending Prayers Upon Him ﷺ

Allah ﷻ ordered us to send prayers upon the Prophet ﷺ but we are certain that we are unable to do anything of our own accord, so instead of attempting to do so we request that Allah ﷻ Himself bestows prayers on the Prophet ﷺ. He called this request of ours prayers from us and said: ***Send prayers and peace upon him in abundance.*** (*Al-Ahzab*, 33:56) In reality, however, these prayers are from Him as we are incapable of sending them ourselves. That is why if we wish to send prayers upon the Prophet ﷺ we say 'O Allah,' or 'O Lord, send prayers upon him.'

If all your good actions were placed on one side of the scale and one prayer from Allah ﷻ was placed on the other, the prayer from Allah ﷻ would outweigh them all. Your actions cannot be compared to the actions of the Lord of the Worlds. In fact were not only your actions, but all the good actions of the whole of creation from the time of Adam to the Day of Judgment placed on one side of the scale and one prayer from the Lord of the Worlds was placed on the other, the prayer from Allah ﷻ would outweigh all those actions. This is one prayer so what about ten prayers that Allah ﷻ bestows in exchange for one prayer upon the Prophet Muhammad ﷺ?

HOW TO SEND PRAYERS UPON HIM AND THEIR EFFECT

Sending prayers upon the Prophet ﷺ strengthens your connection with Allah ﷻ and His Messenger ﷺ since in doing so you are remembering both Allah ﷻ and His Messenger ﷺ. This is especially true if you do it in a state of intense love, longing and veneration. You should be aware while doing so that the source of every blessing which Allah has bestowed upon you and the whole of creation, is Muhammad ﷺ and that his sublime light was the beginning point of creation. In addition, try to picture him ﷺ in front of you while you send prayers upon him ﷺ (especially if you have seen him previously) or picture your shaykh or his blessed *Masjid* or his *Rawdah* or his *Shubbak* (the screen in front of his blessed grave). Send prayers upon him as if you were there until the door is opened to you and the veil is lifted.

If you send prayers upon him in this state it will bring limitless benefits and will bear fruits that none of your actions could bring. It will be a means of purification and will assist you in your journey to Allah ﷻ. If you do not have a shaykh, it will be a cause of you being united with him; if you already have a shaykh, it will strengthen your spiritual connection to him so that the door to the Prophet ﷺ can be opened more swiftly.

The hadith of Ubbay bin Kaʿb [mentioned earlier in the translator's introduction] is sufficient evidence of the benefits of sending prayers upon the Prophet ﷺ.

If someone's worries have been removed and his sins have been forgiven then he has attained felicity in this life and the next. May Allah ﷻ remove our worries and forgive our sins through His Beloved, the healer of our hearts.

THE RELATIONSHIP BETWEEN SENDING PRAYERS UPON THE PROPHET AND CALLING TO ALLAH ﷻ

We must allot a portion of time in which we send prayers upon the Chosen One ﷺ. No one can be a caller to Allah ﷻ if they do not spend some time sending prayers upon the one who first called to Allah ﷻ and guided people to Him. In reality, no-one calls to Allah ﷻ except as a representative and deputy of him ﷺ.

When someone sends prayers upon the Prophet ﷺ and then calls people to Allah ﷻ, a light emanates from his mouth which reaches the people that are listening. The people are thus affected directly by the Prophet ﷺ and by the light of the prayers, not by the speaker himself. Thus if someone sends abundant prayers upon the Prophet ﷺ and then calls people to Allah his words have a great effect on those he is calling.

Those calling to Allah ﷻ have received many openings after repeating the prayer which Sayyiduna Muhammad al-Bakri and others received from the Prophet ﷺ:

ٱللَّٰهُمَّ صَلِّ وَسَلِّمْ وَبَارِكْ عَلَىٰ سَيِّدِنَا مُحَمَّدٍ ٱلْفَاتِحِ لِمَا أُغْلِقَ ٱلْخَاتِمِ
لِمَا سَبَقَ نَاصِرِ ٱلْحَقِّ بِٱلْحَقِّ وَٱلْهَادِي إِلَىٰ صِرَاطِكَ ٱلْمُسْتَقِيمِ
صَلَّى ٱللَّٰهُ عَلَيْهِ وَعَلَىٰ آلِهِ وَصَحْبِهِ حَقَّ قَدْرِهِ وَمِقْدَارِهِ ٱلْعَظِيمِ

Allah ﷻ inspired in the Companions, those that came after them and the knowers of Allah ﷻ, amazing prayers upon the Prophet ﷺ which greatly effect and illuminate the one reading them. You should read a portion of these prayers regularly because they are prayers that emanated from those who are in his presence ﷺ. Those who composed them or received them have knowledge of him which cannot be described and which you cannot come close to. If you pray with the prayers that emanated from their hearts you will receive precious gifts from them. It will be a cause for you to be swiftly brought close and to reach lofty stations. O Allah ﷻ, do not deprive us of all the goodness that You possess because of the evil that we possess!

To illustrate the point, Ḥabīb ʿUmar then read two of Ḥabīb ʿAli al-Habashi's prayers:

ٱللَّٰهُمَّ صَلِّ وَسَلِّمْ عَلَىٰ سَيِّدِنَا مُحَمَّدٍ مِفْتَاحِ بَابِ رَحْمَةِ ٱللَّٰهِ
عَدَدَ مَا فِي عِلْمِ ٱللَّٰهِ صَلَاةً وَسَلَامًا دَائِمَيْنِ بِدَوَامِ مُلْكِ ٱللَّٰهِ
وَعَلَىٰ آلِهِ وَصَحْبِهِ وَسَلِّمْ

ٱللَّٰهُمَّ صَلِّ وَسَلِّمْ وَبَارِكْ عَلَىٰ سَيِّدِنَا مُحَمَّدٍ أَوَّلِ مُتَلَقٍّ لِفَيْضِكَ ٱلْأَوَّلِ
وَأَكْرَمِ حَبِيبٍ تَفَضَّلْتَ عَلَيْهِ فَتَفَضَّلَ وَعَلَىٰ آلِهِ وَصَحْبِهِ وَتَابِعِيهِ
وَحِزْبِهِ مَا دَامَ تَلَقِّيهِ مِنْكَ وَتَرَقِّيهِ إِلَيْكَ وَإِقْبَالُكَ عَلَيْهِ وَإِقْبَالُهُ
عَلَيْكَ وَشُهُودُهُ لَكَ وَانْطِرَاحُهُ لَدَيْكَ صَلَاةً نَشْهَدُكَ بِهَا مِنْ مِرْآتِهِ

وَنَصِلُ بِهَا إِلَىٰ حَضْرَتِكَ مِنْ حَضْرَةِ ذَاتِهِ قَائِمِينَ لَكَ وَلَهُ بِٱلْأَدَبِ ٱلْوَافِرِ مَغْمُورِينَ مِنْكَ وِمِنْهُ بِٱلْمَدَدِ ٱلْبَاطِنِ وَٱلظَّاهِرِ

Shaykh Yusuf bin Ismaʿil al-Nabahani collected many of the prayers of the Knowers of Allah ﷻ. They can be found in *Afḍal al-Salawāt* and *Saʿādat al-Dārayn.*

May Allah ﷻ benefit us by sending prayers upon His Beloved.

TRANSLATION OF THE THREE PRAYERS MENTIONED

1. O Allah, send Your prayers and peace upon our Master Muhammad, the one who opens that which is closed, the seal of those that came before, the defender of truth with truth and the guide to Your straight path (and upon his Family and Companions), in accordance with the greatness of his rank.

2. O Allah, send Your prayers and peace upon our Master Muḥamad, the key to the door of the mercy of Allah, prayers and peace as numerous as that which the knowledge of Allah encompasses, remaining as long as the dominion of Allah remains, and upon his Family and Companions.

3. O Allah, send Your prayers, peace and blessings upon our Master Muhammad, the foremost receiver of your first outpouring, the most noble beloved, upon whom You have bestowed Your favour and he thus excelled; and upon his Family, Companions, his followers and those loyal to him, [prayers, peace and blessings] lasting as long as his receiving from You and his ascent towards You, and Your approach to him and his approach to You, and his witnessing of You and his humble prostration before You.

By this prayer we shall witness You through his mirror and enter into Your presence through his presence, displaying to You and him the best etiquette, fully enveloped in inward and outward spiritual assistance from You and him.

APPENDIX 2

Being with Allah ﷻ and His Messenger ﷺ

Ḥabīb ʿUmar bin Hafīẓ (may Allah protect him and benefit us through him) reflects upon the meaning of being with Allah and His Messenger ﷺ.

Extracts from a lesson in *Ihya ʿUlum al-Din* in Dar al-Mustafa, Tarim, on 9th Rabiʿ al-Awwal 1436 /31st December 2014

The Messenger of Allah ﷺ said: "*A person is with the one they love.*" Thus, you can gauge your love for Allah and His Messenger by gauging how much you are with them.

The Prophet was in the highest state of being with his Lord. For that reason, he said: "*I am nothing but a slave. I eat as a slave eats and I sit as a slave sits.*"

Sayyiduna Ibrahim says in the Qur'an that it is his Lord: "*Who created me, and it is He who guides me; Who gives me food and drink.*" He was constantly with Allah ﷻ, even when he ate and drank.

One of the Knowers of Allah ﷻ said: "*For twenty years people think I have been speaking to them, when in reality I have been speaking to Allah ﷻ.*" If you speak for His sake, in accordance with His Sacred Law and your heart is present with Him, then in reality you are speaking to Him.

The Companions and the pious people of this *Ummah* were constantly with the Messenger of Allah

ﷺ in all their states. One of the Companions repeated three times, addressing the Prophet ﷺ: *"I love Allah and His Messenger!"* He ﷺ replied on each occasion: *"You are with the one you love."*

Sayyiduna Abu'l-ᶜAbbas al-Mursi said: *"If the Prophet ﷺ was absent from me for an instant I would not consider myself a Muslim."*

Ḥabīb ᶜUmar bin ᶜAbd al-Rahman al-ᶜAttas asked: *"How can he be absent from us when he is the source of our existence?"* In other words, without him, we do not exist. Imam al-Haddad said:

وَلِي مِنْ رَسُولِ ٱللهِ جَدِّي عِنَايَةٌ

وَوَجْهٌ وَإِمْدَادٌ وَإِرْثٌ وَإِيثَارُ

'I receive from my grandfather, the Messenger of Allah, care, status, assistance, inheritance & preferential treatment.'

These people reached the highest stations of being with the Beloved ﷺ.

So do not claim to love him and then depart from him. Are you with him in emulating his character? If you truly loved him, you would be with him. Do you think being with him is only in the next life? That which will be manifest in the next life is only that which is stored up in this life. If you want to be with him there, be certain that you have to be with him here.

How long have you been with your lower self (*nafs*)? It calls you to base things while Allah ﷻ and His Messenger ﷺ call you to lofty things. Your lower self calls you to the Fire, while they call you to Paradise. Being with Allah ﷻ and His Messenger ﷺ is better than being with your lower self. Your lower self is the thing which cuts you off most from being with Allah and His Messenger and it is the biggest veil between you and your Lord.

Printed in Great Britain
by Amazon

76981822R00069